P9-DFX-475

INTRODUCTION TO BHAGAVAD-GĪTĀ

Other BBT Publications

Books by His Divine Grace
A.C. Bhaktivedanta Swami Prabhupāda

Bhagavad-gītā As It Is
Śrīmad-Bhāgavatam, Cantos 1-12 (18 vols.)
Śrī Caitanya-caritāmṛta (17 vols.)
Teachings of Lord Caitanya
The Nectar of Devotion
The Nectar of Instruction
Śrī Īśopaniṣad
Easy Journey to Other Planets
Kṛṣṇa Consciousness: The Topmost Yoga System
Kṛṣṇa, the Supreme Personality of Godhead
Perfect Questions, Perfect Answers
Teachings of Lord Kapila
Teachings of Queen Kuntī
The Path of Perfection
Kṛṣṇa, the Reservoir of Pleasure
The Science of Self-Realization
The Journey of Self-Discovery
A Second Chance: The Story of a Near-Death Experience
Preaching is the Essence
Life Comes From Life
The Perfection of Yoga
Beyond Birth and Death
On the Way to Kṛṣṇa
Message of Godhead
Back to Godhead magazine (founder)

Available from:

The Bhaktivedanta Book Trust
3764 Watseka Ave.
Los Angeles,
CA 90034, USA

The Bhaktivedanta Book Trust
P.O..Box 324
Borehamwood, Hetrs.
WD6 1NB, U.K.

The Bhaktivedanta Book Trust
P.O. Box 262
Botany, N.S.W
2019 Australia

ALL GLORY TO ŚRĪ GURU AND GAURĀṄGA

INTRODUCTION TO BHAGAVAD-GĪTĀ

His Divine Grace

A. C. BHAKTIVEDANTA SWAMI PRABHUPĀDA

Founder-Ācārya of the International Society for Kṛṣṇa Consciousness

THE BHAKTIVEDANTA BOOK TRUST

Readers interested in the subject matter of this book are invited to correspond with the Secretary (for a full list in each country please see the back of this book):

International Society for Krishna Consciousness
3764 Watseka Avenue, Los Angeles,
California 90034, USA

International Society for Krishna Consciousness
P.O. Box 324, Borehamwood, Herts.,
WD6 1NB, U.K.

International Society for Krishna Consciousness
P.O. Box 159, Kings Cross,
N.S.W. 2011, Australia

First Printing, 1968 5,000
Second Printing, 1992 100,000
Third Printing, 1994 100,000
Fourth Printing, 2003 100,000

© 1992 The Bhaktivedanta Book Trust reg.
All Rights Reserved
Printed in the United States of America

ISBN: 0-89213-293-0

Preface

The Bhagavad-gītā is the greatest of India's ancient spiritual classics. Śrīla Prabhupāda, the Founder-Ācārya of the International Society for Krishna Consciousness, originally translated the Bhagavad-gītā in 1967, providing each verse with an illuminating commentary. Having only recently come to the West, he was unable to print the book at that time. Therefore, the introduction which he had written for the Bhagavad-gītā was printed first as a separate pamphlet. This booklet is a reprint of that introduction. The reader will find in it a thorough exposition of the philosophy of the Bhagavad-gītā in a clear and straightforward manner. This introduction is important for those who are approaching the Bhagavad-gītā for the first time. Unlike other presentations and translations, Śrīla Prabhupāda presents the Bhagavad-gītā as it is, free from personal speculations and interpretations. He focuses our attention on what Kṛṣṇa is actually teaching in the Gītā. For all these reasons we are sure you will find this introduction to the Bhagavad-gītā to be enlightening and conducive to personal transformation.

The Publishers

Bhagavad-gītā is also known as *Gītopaniṣad*. It is the essence of Vedic knowledge and one of the most important *Upaniṣads* in Vedic literature. Of course there are many commentaries in English on the *Bhagavad-gītā*, and one may question the necessity for another one. This present edition can be explained in the following way. Recently an American lady asked me to recommend an English translation of *Bhagavad-gītā*. Of course in America there are so many editions of *Bhagavad-gītā* available in English, but as far as I have seen, not only in America but also in India, none of them can be strictly said to be authoritative because in almost every one of them the commentator has expressed his own opinions without touching the spirit of *Bhagavad-gītā* as it is.

The spirit of *Bhagavad-gītā* is mentioned in *Bhagavad-gītā* itself. It is just like this: If we want to take a particular medicine, then we have to follow the directions written on the label. We cannot take the medicine according to our own whim or the direction of a friend. It must be taken according to the directions on the label or the directions given by a physician. Similarly, *Bhagavad-gītā* should be taken or accepted as it is directed by the speaker Himself. The speaker of *Bhagavad-gītā* is Lord Śrī Kṛṣṇa. He is mentioned on every page of *Bhagavad-gītā* as the Supreme Personality of Godhead, Bhagavān. Of course the word *bhagavān* sometimes refers to any powerful person or any powerful demigod, and certainly here *bhagavān* designates Lord Śrī Kṛṣṇa as a great personality, but at the same time we should know that Lord Śrī

Kṛṣṇa is the Supreme Personality of Godhead, as is confirmed by all great *ācāryas* (spiritual masters) like Śaṅkarācārya, Rāmānujācārya, Madhvācārya, Nimbārka Svāmī, Śrī Caitanya Mahāprabhu and many other authorities of Vedic knowledge in India. The Lord Himself also establishes Himself as the Supreme Personality of Godhead in the *Bhagavad-gītā*, and He is accepted as such in the *Brahma-saṁhitā* and all the *Purāṇas*, especially the *Śrīmad-Bhāgavatam*, known as the *Bhāgavata Purāṇa (kṛṣṇas tu bhagavān svayam)*. Therefore we should take *Bhagavad-gītā* as it is directed by the Personality of Godhead Himself.

In the Fourth Chapter of the *Gītā* (4.1–3) the Lord says:

imaṁ vivasvate yogaṁ
proktavān aham avyayam
vivasvān manave prāha
manur ikṣvākave 'bravīt

evaṁ paramparā-prāptam
imaṁ rājarṣayo viduḥ
sa kāleneha mahatā
yogo naṣṭaḥ parantapa

sa evāyaṁ mayā te 'dya
yogaḥ proktaḥ purātanaḥ
bhakto 'si me sakhā ceti
rahasyaṁ hy etad uttamam

Here the Lord informs Arjuna that this system of *yoga*, the *Bhagavad-gītā*, was first spoken to the sun-god, and the sun-god explained it to Manu, and Manu explained it to Ikṣvāku, and in that way, by disciplic succession, one speaker after another, this *yoga* system has been coming down. But in the course of time it has become lost. Consequently the Lord has to speak it again, this time to Arjuna on the Battlefield of Kurukṣetra.

He tells Arjuna that He is relating this supreme secret to him because Arjuna is His devotee and His friend. The purport of this is that *Bhagavad-gītā* is a treatise which is especially meant for the devotee of the Lord. There are three classes of tran-scendentalists, namely the *jñānī*, the *yogī* and the *bhakta*, or the impersonalist, the meditator and the devotee. Here the Lord clearly tells Arjuna that He is making him the first receiver of a new *paramparā* (disciplic succession) because the old succession was broken. It was the Lord's wish, therefore, to establish another *paramparā* in the same line of thought that was coming down from the sun-god to others, and it was His wish that His teaching be distributed anew by Arjuna. He wanted Arjuna to become the authority in understanding the *Bhagavad-gītā.* So we see that *Bhagavad-gītā* is instructed to Arjuna especially because Arjuna was a devotee of the Lord, a direct student of Kṛṣṇa, and His intimate friend. Therefore *Bhagavad-gītā* is best understood by a person who has qualities similar to Arjuna's. That is to say he must be a devotee in a direct relationship with the Lord. As soon as one becomes a devotee of the Lord, he also has a direct relationship with the Lord. That is a very elaborate subject matter, but briefly it can be stated that a devotee is in a relationship with the Supreme Personality of Godhead in one of five different ways:

1. One may be a devotee in a passive state;
2. One may be a devotee in an active state;
3. One may be a devotee as a friend;
4. One may be a devotee as a parent;
5. One may be a devotee as a conjugal lover.

Arjuna was in a relationship with the Lord as friend. Of course there is a gulf of difference between this friendship and the friendship found in the material world. This is transcendental friendship, which cannot be had by everyone. Of course everyone has a particular relationship with the Lord, and that relationship is evoked by the perfection of devotional service. But in the present status of our life, not only have we forgotten the Supreme Lord, but we have forgotten our eternal relationship with the Lord. Every living being, out of the many, many billions and trillions of living beings, has a particular relationship with the Lord eternally. That is called *svarūpa.* By the process of devotional service, one can revive that *svarūpa,* and that stage is called *svarūpa-siddhi*—perfection of one's constitutional position. So Arjuna was a devotee, and he was in touch with the Supreme Lord in friendship.

How Arjuna accepted this *Bhagavad-gītā* should be noted. His manner of acceptance is given in the Tenth Chapter (10.12–14):

arjuna uvāca
paraṁ brahma paraṁ dhāma
pavitraṁ paramaṁ bhavān

puruṣaṁ śāśvataṁ divyam
ādi-devam ajaṁ vibhum

āhus tvām ṛṣayaḥ sarve
devarṣir nāradas tathā
asito devalo vyāsaḥ
svayaṁ caiva bravīṣi me

sarvam etad ṛtaṁ manye
yan māṁ vadasi keśava
na hi te bhagavan vyaktiṁ
vidur devā na dānavāḥ

"Arjuna said: You are the Supreme Personality of Godhead, the ultimate abode, the purest, the Absolute Truth. You are the eternal, transcendental, original person, the unborn, the greatest. All the great sages such as Nārada, Asita, Devala, and Vyāsa confirm this truth about You, and now You Yourself are declaring it to me. O Kṛṣṇa, I totally accept as truth all that You have told me. Neither the demigods nor the demons, O Lord, can understand Your personality."

After hearing *Bhagavad-gītā* from the Supreme Personality of Godhead, Arjuna accepted Kṛṣṇa as *paraṁ brahma,* the Supreme Brahman. Every living being is Brahman, but the supreme living being, or the Supreme Personality of Godhead, is the Supreme Brahman. *Paraṁ dhāma* means that He is the supreme rest or abode of everything; *pavitram* means that He is pure, untainted by material contamination; *puruṣam* means that He is the supreme enjoyer; *śāśvatam,* original; *divyam,* transcendental; *ādi-devam,* the Supreme Personality of Godhead; *ajam,* the unborn; and *vibhum,* the greatest.

Now one may think that because Kṛṣṇa was the friend of Arjuna, Arjuna was telling Him all this by way of flattery, but Arjuna, just to drive out this kind of doubt from the minds of the readers of *Bhagavad-gītā,* substantiates these praises in the next verse when he says that Kṛṣṇa is accepted as the Supreme Personality of Godhead not only by himself but by authorities like Nārada, Asita, Devala and Vyāsadeva. These are great personalities who distribute the Vedic knowledge as it is accepted by all *ācāryas.* Therefore Arjuna tells Kṛṣṇa that he accepts whatever He says to be completely perfect. *Sarvam etad ṛtaṁ manye:* "I accept everything You say to be true." Arjuna also says that the personality of the Lord is very difficult to understand and that He cannot be known even by the great demigods. This means that the Lord cannot even be known by personalities greater than human beings. So how can a human being understand Lord Śrī Kṛṣṇa without becoming His devotee?

Therefore *Bhagavad-gītā* should be taken up in a spirit of devotion. One should not think that he is equal to Kṛṣṇa, nor should he think that Kṛṣṇa is an ordinary personality or even a very great personality. Lord Śrī Kṛṣṇa is the Supreme Personality of Godhead. So according to the statements of *Bhagavad-gītā* or the statements of Arjuna, the person who is trying to understand the *Bhagavad-gītā,* we should at least theoretically accept Śrī Kṛṣṇa as the Supreme Personality of Godhead, and with that submissive spirit we can understand the *Bhagavad-gītā*. Unless one reads the *Bhagavad-gītā* in a submissive spirit, it is very difficult to understand *Bhagavad-gītā*, because it is a great mystery.

Just what is the *Bhagavad-gītā?* The purpose of *Bhagavad-gītā* is to deliver mankind from the nescience of material existence. Every man is in difficulty in so many ways, as Arjuna also was in difficulty in having to fight the Battle of Kurukṣetra. Arjuna surrendered unto Śrī Kṛṣṇa, and consequently this *Bhagavad-gītā* was spoken. Not only Arjuna, but every one of us is full of anxieties because of this material existence. Our very existence is in the atmosphere of nonexistence. Actually we are not meant to be threatened by nonexistence. Our existence is eternal. But somehow or other we are put into *asat*. *Asat* refers to that which does not exist.

Out of so many human beings who are suffering, there are a few who are actually inquiring about their position, as to what they are, why they are put into this awkward position and so on. Unless one is awakened to this position of questioning his suffering, unless he realizes that he doesn't want suffering but rather wants to make a solution to all suffering, then one is not to be considered a perfect human being. Humanity begins when this sort of inquiry is awakened in one's mind. In the *Brahma-sūtra* this inquiry is called *brahma jijñāsā*. *Athāto brahma jijñāsā*. Every activity of the human being is to be considered a failure unless he inquires about the nature of the Absolute. Therefore those who begin to question why they are suffering or where they came from and where they shall go after death are proper students for understanding *Bhagavad-gītā*. The sincere student should also have a firm respect for the Supreme Personality of Godhead. Such a student was Arjuna.

Lord Kṛṣṇa descends specifically to reestablish the real purpose of life when man forgets that purpose. Even then, out of many, many human beings who awaken, there may be one who actually enters the spirit of understanding his position, and for him this *Bhagavad-gītā* is spoken. Actually we are all swallowed by the tigress of nescience, but the Lord is very merciful upon living entities, especially human beings. To this end He spoke the *Bhagavad-gītā*, making His friend Arjuna His student.

Being an associate of Lord Kṛṣṇa, Arjuna was above all ignorance, but Arjuna was put into ignorance on the Battlefield of Kurukṣetra just to question Lord Kṛṣṇa about the problems of life so that the Lord could explain them for the benefit of future generations of human beings and chalk out the plan of life. Then man could act accordingly and perfect the mission of human life.

The subject of the *Bhagavad-gītā* entails the comprehension of five basic truths. First of all, the science of God is explained and then the constitutional position of the living entities, *jīvas*. There is *īśvara*, which means the controller, and there are jīvas, the living entities which are controlled. If a living entity says that he is not controlled but that he is free, then he is insane. The living being is controlled in every respect, at least in his conditioned life. So in the *Bhagavad-gītā* the subject matter deals with the *īśvara*, the supreme controller, and the *jīvas*, the controlled living entities. *Prakṛti* (material nature) and time (the duration of existence of the whole universe or the manifestation of material nature) and karma (activity) are also discussed. The cosmic manifestation is full of different activities. All living entities are engaged in different activities. From *Bhagavad-gītā* we must learn what God is, what the living entities are, what *prakṛti* is, what the cosmic manifestation is, how it is controlled by time, and what the activities of the living entities are.

Out of these five basic subject matters in *Bhagavad-gītā* it is established that the Supreme Godhead, or Kṛṣṇa, or Brahman, or the supreme controller, or Paramātmā—you may use whatever name you like—is the greatest of all. The living beings are in quality like the supreme controller. For instance, the Lord has control over the universal affairs of material nature, as will be explained in the later chapters of *Bhagavad-gītā*. Material nature is not independent. She is acting under the directions of the Supreme Lord. As Lord Kṛṣṇa says, *mayādhyakṣeṇa prakṛtiḥ sūyate sa-carācaram:* "This material nature is working under My direction." When we see wonderful things happening in the cosmic nature, we should know that behind this cosmic manifestation there is a controller. Nothing could be manifested without being controlled. It is childish not to consider the controller. For instance, a child may think that an automobile is quite wonderful to be able to run without a horse or other animal pulling it, but a sane man knows the nature of the automobile's engineering arrangement. He always knows that behind the machinery there is a man, a driver. Similarly, the Supreme Lord is the driver under whose direction everything is working. Now the *jīvas,* or the living entities, have been accepted by the Lord, as we will note in the later chapters, as His parts and parcels. A particle of gold is also gold, a drop of water from the ocean is also salty, and similarly we the living entities, being part and parcel of the supreme controller, *īśvara,* or Bhagavān, Lord Śrī Kṛṣṇa, have all the qualities of the Supreme Lord in minute quantity because we are minute *īśvaras,* subordinate *īśvaras.* We are trying to control nature, as presently we are trying to control space or planets, and this tendency to control is there because it is in Kṛṣṇa. But although we have a tendency to lord it over material nature, we should know that we are not the supreme controller. This is explained in *Bhagavad-gītā.*

What is material nature? This is also explained in *Gītā* as inferior *prakṛti,* inferior nature. The living entity is explained as the superior *prakṛti. Prakṛti* is always under control, whether inferior or superior. *Prakṛti* is female, and she is controlled by the Lord just as the activities of a wife are controlled by the husband. *Prakṛti* is always subordinate, predominated by the Lord, who is the predominator. The living entities and material nature are both predominated, controlled by the Supreme Lord. According to the *Gītā,* the living entities, although parts and parcels of the Supreme

Lord, are to be considered *prakṛti.* This is clearly mentioned in the Seventh Chapter of *Bhagavad-gītā. Apareyam itas tv anyāṁ prakṛtiṁ viddhi me parām/ jīva-bhūtām:* "This material nature is My inferior *prakṛti,* but beyond this is another *prakṛti—jīva-bhūtām,* the living entity."

Material nature itself is constituted by three qualities: the mode of goodness, the mode of passion and the mode of ignorance. Above these modes there is eternal time, and by a combination of these modes of nature and under the control and purview of eternal time there are activities, which are called *karma.* These activities are being carried out from time immemorial, and we are suffering or enjoying the fruits of our activities. For instance, suppose I am a businessman and have worked very hard with intelligence and have amassed a great bank balance. Then I am an enjoyer. But then say I have lost all my money in business; then I am a sufferer. Similarly, in every field of life we enjoy the results of our work, or we suffer the results. This is called *karma.*

Īśvara (the Supreme Lord), *jīva* (the living entity), *prakṛti* (nature), *kāla* (eternal time) and *karma* (activity) are all explained in the *Bhagavad-gītā.* Out of these five, the Lord, the living entities, material nature and time are eternal. The manifestation of *prakṛti* may be temporary, but it is not false. Some philosophers say that the manifestation of material nature is false, but according to the philosophy of *Bhagavad-gītā* or according to the philosophy of the Vaiṣṇavas, this is not so. The manifestation of the world is not accepted as false; it is accepted as real, but temporary. It is likened unto a cloud which moves across the sky, or the coming of the rainy season, which nourishes grains. As soon as the rainy season is over and as soon as the cloud goes away, all the crops which were nourished by the rain dry up. Similarly, this material manifestation takes place at a certain interval, stays for a while and then disappears. Such are the workings of *prakṛti.* But this cycle is working eternally. Therefore *prakṛtī* is eternal; it is not false. The Lord refers to this as "My *prakṛti.*" This material nature is the separated energy of the Supreme Lord, and similarly the living entities are also the energy of the Supreme Lord, although they are not separated but eternally related. So the Lord, the living entity, material nature and time are all interrelated and are all eternal. However, the other item, *karma,* is not eternal. The effects of *karma* may be very old indeed. We are suffering or enjoying the results of our activities from time immemorial, but we can change the results of our *karma,* or our activity, and this change depends on the perfection of our knowledge. We are engaged in various activities. Undoubtedly we do not know what sort of activities we should adopt to gain relief from the actions and reactions of all these activities, but this is also explained in the *Bhagavad-gītā.*

The position of *īśvara,* the Supreme Lord, is that of supreme consciousness. The *jīvas,* or the living entities, being parts and parcels of the Supreme Lord, are also conscious. Both the living entity and material nature are explained as *prakṛti,* the energy of the Supreme Lord, but one of the two, the *jīva,* is conscious. The other *prakṛti* is not conscious. That is the difference. Therefore the *jīva-prakṛti* is called superior because the *jīva* has consciousness which is similar to the Lord's. The Lord's is supreme consciousness, however, and one should not claim that the *jīva,* the living entity, is also supremely conscious. The living being cannot be supremely conscious at any stage of his perfection, and the theory that he can be so is a misleading theory. Conscious he may be, but he is not perfectly or supremely conscious.

The distinction between the *jīva* and the *īśvara* will be explained in the Thirteenth Chapter of *Bhagavad-gītā.* The Lord is *kṣetra-jña,* conscious, as is the living being, but the living being is conscious of his particular body, whereas the Lord is conscious of all bodies. Because He lives in the heart of every living being, He is conscious of the psychic movements of the particular *jīvas.* We should not forget this. It is also explained that the Paramātmā, the Supreme Personality of Godhead, is living in everyone's heart as *īśvara,* as the controller, and that He is giving directions for the living entity to act as he desires. The living entity forgets what to do. First of all he makes a determination to act in a certain way, and then he is entangled in the actions and reactions of his own *karma.* After giving up one type of body, he enters another type of body, as we put on and take off clothes. As the soul thus migrates, he suffers the actions and reactions of his past activities. These activities can be changed when the living being is in the mode of goodness, in sanity, and understands what sort of activities he should adopt. If he does so, then all the actions and reactions of his past activities can be changed. Consequently, *karma* is not eternal. Therefore we stated that of the five items (*īśvara, jīva, prakṛtī,* time and *karma*) four are eternal, whereas *karma* is not eternal.

The supreme conscious *īśvara* is similar to the living entity in this way: both the consciousness of the Lord and that of the living entity are transcendental. It is not that consciousness is generated by the association of matter. That is a mistaken idea. The theory that consciousness develops under certain circumstances of material combination is not accepted in the *Bhagavad-gītā.* Consciousness may be pervertedly reflected by the covering of material circumstances, just as light reflected through colored glass may appear to be a certain color, but the consciousness of the Lord is not materially affected. Lord Kṛṣṇa says, *mayādhyakṣeṇa prakṛtiḥ.* When He descends into the material universe, His consciousness is not materially affected. If He were so affected, He would be unfit to speak on transcendental matters as He does in the *Bhagavad-gītā.* One cannot say anything about the transcendental world without being free from materially contaminated consciousness. So the Lord is not materially contaminated. Our consciousness, at the present moment, however, *is* materially contaminated. The *Bhagavad-gītā* teaches that we have to purify this materially contaminated consciousness. In pure consciousness, our actions will be dovetailed to the will of *īśvara,* and that will make us happy. It is not that we have to cease all activities. Rather, our activities are to be purified, and purified activities are called *bhakti.* Activities in *bhakti* appear to be like ordinary activities, but they are not contaminated. An ignorant person may see that a devotee is acting or working like an ordinary man, but such a person with a poor fund of knowledge does not know that the activities of the devotee or of the Lord are not contaminated by impure consciousness or matter. They are transcendental to the three modes of nature. We should know, however, that at this point our consciousness is contaminated.

When we are materially contaminated, we are called conditioned. False consciousness is exhibited under the impression that I am a product of material nature. This is called false ego. One who is absorbed in the thought of bodily conceptions cannot understand his situation. *Bhagavad-gītā* was spoken to liberate one from the bodily conception of life, and Arjuna put himself in this position in order to receive this information from the Lord. One must become free from the bodily conception of life; that is the preliminary activity for the transcendentalist. One who wants to become free, who wants to become liberated, must first of all learn that he is not this material body. *Mukti,* or liberation, means freedom from material consciousness. In the *Śrīmad-Bhāgavatam* also the definition of liberation is given. *Muktir hitvānyathā-rūpaṁ svarūpeṇa vyavasthitiḥ: mukti* means liberation from the contaminated consciousness of this material world and situation in pure consciousness. All the instructions of *Bhagavad-gītā* are intended to awaken this pure consciousness, and therefore we find at the last stage of the *Gītā's* instructions that Kṛṣṇa is asking Arjuna whether he is now in purified consciousness. Purified consciousness means acting in accordance with the instructions of the Lord. This is the whole sum and substance of purified consciousness. Consciousness is already there because we are part and parcel of the Lord, but for us there is the affinity of being affected by the inferior modes. But the Lord, being the Supreme, is never affected. That is the difference between the Supreme Lord and the small individual souls.

What is this consciousness? This conscious-ness is "I am." Then what am I? In contaminated consciousness "I am" means "I am the lord of all I survey. I am the enjoyer." The world revolves because every living being thinks that he is the lord and creator of the material world. Material consciousness has two psychic divisions. One is that I am the creator, and the other is that I am the enjoyer. But actually the Supreme Lord is both the creator and the enjoyer, and the living entity, being part and parcel of the Supreme Lord, is neither the creator nor the enjoyer, but a cooperator. He is the created and the enjoyed. For instance, a part of a machine cooperates with the whole machine; a part of the body cooperates with the whole body. The hands, legs, eyes, and so on are all parts of the body, but they are not actually the enjoyers. The stomach is the enjoyer. The legs move, the hands supply food, the teeth chew, and all parts of the body are engaged in satisfying the stomach because the stomach is the principal factor that nourishes the body's organization. Therefore everything is given to the stomach. One nourishes the tree by watering its root, and one nourishes the body by feeding the stomach, for if the body is to be kept in a healthy state, then the parts of the body must cooperate to feed the stomach. Similarly, the Supreme Lord is the enjoyer and the creator, and we, as subordinate living beings, are meant to cooperate to satisfy Him. This cooperation will actually help us, just as food taken by the stomach will help all other parts of the body. If the fingers of the hand think that they should take the food themselves instead of giving it to the stomach, then they will be frustrated. The central figure of creation and of enjoyment is the Supreme Lord, and the living entities are cooperators. By cooperation they enjoy. The relation is also like that of the master and the servant. If the master is fully satisfied, then the servant is satisfied. Similarly, the Supreme Lord should be satisfied, although the tendency to become the creator and the tendency to enjoy the material world are there also in the living entities because these tendencies are there in the Supreme Lord who has created the manifested cosmic world.

We shall find, therefore, in this *Bhagavad-gītā* that the complete whole is comprised of the supreme controller, the controlled living entities, the cosmic manifestation, eternal time and *karma*, or activities, and all of these are explained in this text. All of these taken completely form the complete whole, and the complete whole is called the Supreme Absolute Truth. The complete whole and the complete Absolute Truth are the complete Personality of Godhead, Śrī Kṛṣṇa. All manifestations are due to His different energies. He is the complete whole.

It is also explained in the *Gītā* that impersonal Brahman is also subordinate to the complete Supreme Person (*brahmaṇo hi pratiṣṭhāham*). Brahman is more explicitly explained in the *Brahma-sūtra* to be like the rays of the sunshine. The impersonal Brahman is the shining rays of the Supreme Personality of Godhead. Impersonal Brahman is incomplete realization of the absolute whole, and so also is the conception of Paramātmā. In the Fifteenth Chapter it shall be seen that the Supreme Personality of Godhead, Puruṣottama, is above both impersonal Brahman and the partial realization of Paramātmā. The Supreme Personality of Godhead is called *sac-cid-ānanda-vigraha*. The *Brahma-saṁhitā* begins in this way: *īśvaraḥ paramaḥ kṛṣṇaḥ sac-cid-ānanda-vigrahaḥ/ anādir ādir govindaḥ sarva-kāraṇa-kāraṇam*. "Govinda, Kṛṣṇa, is the cause of all causes. He is the primal cause, and He is the very form of eternity, knowledge and bliss." Impersonal Brahman realization is the realization of His *sat* (eternity) feature. Paramātmā realization is the realization of *sat-cit* (eternal knowledge). But realization of the Personality of Godhead, Kṛṣṇa, is realization of all the transcendental features: *sat, cīt and ānanda* (eternity, knowledge, and bliss) in complete *vigraha* (form).

People with less intelligence consider the Supreme Truth to be impersonal, but He is a transcendental person, and this is confirmed in all Vedic literatures. *Nityo nityānāṁ cetanaś cetanānām.* (*Kaṭha Upaniṣad* 2.2.13) As we are all individual living beings and have our individuality, the Supreme Absolute Truth is also, in the ultimate issue, a person, and realization of the Personality of Godhead is realization of all of the transcendental features in His complete form. The complete whole is not formless. If He is formless, or if He is less than any other thing, then He cannot be the complete whole. The complete whole must have everything within our experience and beyond our experience, otherwise it cannot be complete.

The complete whole, Personality of Godhead, has immense potencies (*parāsya śaktir vividhaiva śrūyate*). How Kṛṣṇa is acting in different potencies is also explained in *Bhagavad-gītā*. This phenomenal world or material world in which we are placed is also complete in itself because the twenty-four elements of which this material universe is a temporary manifestation, according to Sāṅkhya philosophy, are completely adjusted to produce complete resources which are necessary for the maintenance and subsistence of this universe. There is nothing extraneous, nor is there anything needed. This manifestation has its own time fixed by the energy of the supreme whole, and when its time is complete, these temporary manifestations will be annihilated by the complete arrangement of the complete. There is complete facility for the small complete units, namely the living entities, to realize the complete, and all sorts of incompleteness are experienced due to incomplete knowledge of the complete. So *Bhagavad-gītā* contains the complete knowledge of Vedic wisdom.

All Vedic knowledge is infallible, and Hindus accept Vedic knowledge to be complete and infallible. For example, cow dung is the stool of an animal, and according to *smṛti,* or Vedic injunction, if one touches the stool of an animal he has to take a bath to purify himself. But in the Vedic scriptures cow dung is considered to be a purifying agent. One might consider this to be contradictory, but it is accepted because it is Vedic injunction, and indeed by accepting this, one will not commit a mistake; subsequently it has been proved by modern science that cow dung contains all antiseptic properties. So Vedic knowledge is complete because it is above all doubts and mistakes, and *Bhagavad-gītā* is the essence of all Vedic knowledge.

Vedic knowledge is not a question of research. Our research work is imperfect because we are researching things with imperfect senses. We have to accept perfect knowledge which comes down, as is stated in *Bhagavad-gītā*, by the *paramparā* (disciplic succession). We have to receive knowledge from the proper source in disciplic succession beginning with the supreme spiritual master, the Lord Himself, and handed down to a succession of spiritual masters. Arjuna, the student who took lessons from Lord Śrī Kṛṣṇa, accepts everything that He says without contradicting Him. One is not allowed to accept one portion of

Bhagavad-gītā and not another. No. We must accept *Bhagavad-gītā* without interpretation, without deletion and without our own whimsical participation in the matter. The *Gītā* should be taken as the most perfect presentation of Vedic knowledge. Vedic knowledge is received from transcendental sources, and the first words were spoken by the Lord Himself. The words spoken by the Lord are called *apauruṣeya*, meaning that they are different from words spoken by a person of the mundane world who is infected with four defects. A mundaner (1) is sure to commit mistakes, (2) is invariably illusioned, (3) has the tendency to cheat others and (4) is limited by imperfect senses. With these four imperfections, one cannot deliver perfect information of all-pervading knowledge.

Vedic knowledge is not imparted by such defective living entities. It was imparted unto the heart of Brahmā, the first created living being, and Brahmā in his turn disseminated this knowledge to his sons and disciples, as he originally received it from the Lord. The Lord is *pūrṇam*, all-perfect, and there is no possibility of His becoming subjected to the laws of material nature. One should therefore be intelligent enough to know that the Lord is the only proprietor of everything in the universe and that He is the original creator, the creator of Brahmā. In the Eleventh Chapter the Lord is addressed as *prapitāmaha* because Brahmā is addressed as *pitāmaha*, the grandfather, and He is the creator of the grandfather. So no one should claim to be the proprietor of anything; one should accept only things which are set aside for him by the Lord as his quota for his maintenance.

There are many examples given of how we are to utilize those things which are set aside for us by the Lord. This is also explained in *Bhagavad-gītā.* In the beginning, Arjuna decided that he should not fight in the Battle of Kurukṣetra. This was his own decision. Arjuna told the Lord that it was not possible for him to enjoy the kingdom after killing his own kinsmen. This decision was based on the body because he was thinking that the body was himself and that his bodily relations or expansions were his brothers, nephews, brothers-in-law, grandfathers and so on. Therefore he wanted to satisfy his bodily demands. *Bhagavad-gītā* was spoken by the Lord just to change this view, and at the end Arjuna decides to fight under the directions of the Lord when he says, *kariṣye vacanaṁ tava:* "I shall act according to Your word."

In this world men are not meant for quarreling like cats and dogs. Men must be intelligent to realize the importance of human life and refuse to act like ordinary animals. A human being should realize the aim of his life, and this direction is given in all Vedic literatures, and the essence is given in *Bhagavad-gītā.* Vedic literature is meant for human beings, not for animals. Animals can kill other living animals, and there is no question of sin on their part, but if a man kills an animal for the satisfaction of his uncontrolled taste, he must be responsible for breaking the laws of nature. In the *Bhagavad-gītā* it is clearly explained that there are three kinds of activities according to the different modes of nature: the activities of goodness, of passion and of ignorance. Similarly, there are three kinds of eatables also: eatables in goodness, passion and ignorance. All of this is clearly described, and if we properly utilize the instructions of *Bhagavad-gītā*, then our whole life will become purified, and ultimately we will be able to reach the destination which is beyond this material sky.

That destination is called the *sanātana* sky, the eternal, spiritual sky. In this material world we find that everything is temporary. It comes into being, stays for some time, produces some by-products, dwindles and then vanishes. That is the law of the material world, whether we use as an example this body, or a piece of fruit or anything. But beyond this temporary world there is another world of which we have information. That world consists of another nature, which is *sanātana*, eternal. *Jīva* is also described as *sanātana*, eternal, and the Lord is also described as *sanātana* in the Eleventh Chapter. We have an intimate relationship with the Lord, and because we are all qualitatively one—the *sanātana-dhāma*, or sky, the *sanātana* Supreme Personality and the *sanātana* living entities—the whole purpose of *Bhagavad-gītā* is to revive our *sanātana* occupation, or *sanātana-dharma*, which is the eternal occupation of the living entity. We are temporarily engaged in different activities, but all of these activities can be purified when we give up all these temporary activities and take up the activities which are prescribed by the Supreme Lord. That is called our pure life.

The Supreme Lord and His transcendental abode are both *sanātana*, as are the living entities, and the combined association of the Supreme Lord and the living entities in the *sanātana* abode is the perfection of human life. The Lord is very kind to the living entities because they are His sons. Lord Kṛṣṇa declares in *Bhagavad-gītā, sarva-yoniṣu... ahaṁ bīja-pradaḥ pitā:* "I am the father of all." Of course there are all types of living entities according to their various *karmas,* but here the Lord claims that He is the father of all of them. Therefore the Lord descends to reclaim all of these fallen, conditioned souls, to call them back to the *sanātana* eternal sky so that the *sanātana* living entities may regain their eternal *sanātana* positions in eternal association with the Lord. The Lord comes Himself in different incarnations, or He sends His confidential servants as sons or His associates or *ācāryas* to reclaim the conditioned souls.

Therefore, *sanātana-dharma* does not refer to any sectarian process of religion. It is the eternal function of the eternal living entities in relationship with the eternal Supreme Lord. *Sanātana-dharma* refers, as stated previously, to the eternal occupation of the living entity. Śrīpāda Rāmānujācārya has explained the word *sanātana* as "that which has neither beginning nor end," so when we speak of *sanātana-dharma,* we must take it for granted on the authority of Śrīpāda Rāmānujācārya that it has neither beginning nor end.

The English world religion is a little different from *sanātana-dharma.* Religion conveys the idea of faith, and faith may change. One may have faith in a particular process, and he may change this faith and adopt another, but *sanātana-dharma* refers to that activity which cannot be changed. For instance, liquidity cannot be taken from water, nor can heat be taken from fire. Similarly, the eternal function of the eternal living entity cannot be taken from the living entity. *Sanātana-dharma* is eternally integral with the living entity. When we speak of *sanātana-dharma,* therefore, we must take it for granted on the authority of Śrīpāda Rāmānujācārya that it has neither beginning nor end. That which has neither end nor beginning must not be sectarian, for it cannot be limited by any boundaries. Those belonging to some sectarian faith will wrongly consider that *sanātana-dharma* is also sectarian, but if we go deeply into the matter and consider it in the light of modern science, it is possible for us to see that *sanātana-dharma* is the business of all the people of the world—nay, of all the living entities of the universe.

Non-*sanātana* religious faith may have some beginning in the annals of human history, but there is no beginning to the history of *sanātana-dharma,* because it remains eternally with the living entities. Insofar as the living entities are concerned, the authoritative *śāstras* state that the living entity has neither birth nor death. In the *Gītā* it is stated that the living entity is never born and he never dies. He is eternal and indestructible, and he continues to live after the destruction of his temporary material body. In reference to the concept of *sanātana-dharma,* we must try to understand the concept of religion from the Sanskrit root meaning of the word. *Dharma* refers to that which is constantly existing with a particular object. We conclude that there is heat and light along with the fire; without heat and light, there is no meaning to the word fire. Similarly, we must discover the essential part of the living being, that part which is his constant companion. That constant companion is his eternal quality, and that eternal quality is his eternal religion.

When Sanātana Gosvāmī asked Śrī Caitanya Mahāprabhu about the *svarūpa* of every living being, the Lord replied that the *svarūpa,* or constitutional position, of the living being is the rendering of service to the Supreme Personality of Godhead. If we analyze this statement of Lord Caitanya's, we can easily see that every living being is constantly engaged in rendering service to another living being. A living being serves other living beings in various capacities. By doing so, the living entity enjoys life. The lower animals serve human beings as servants serve their master. A serves B master, B serves C master, and C serves D master and so on. Under these circumstances, we can see that one friend serves another friend, the mother serves the son, the wife serves the husband, the husband serves the wife and so on. If we go on searching in this spirit, it will be seen that there is no exception in the society of living beings to the activity of service. The politician presents his manifesto for the public to convince them of his capacity for service. The voters therefore give the politician their valuable votes, thinking that he will render valuable service to society. The shopkeeper serves the customer, and the artisan serves the capitalist. The capitalist serves the family, and the family serves the state in the terms of the eternal capacity of the eternal living being. In this way we can see that no living being is exempt from rendering service to other living beings, and therefore we can safely conclude that service is the constant companion of the living being and that the rendering of service is the eternal religion of the living being.

Yet man professes to belong to a particular type of faith with reference to particular time and circumstance and thus claims to be a Hindu, Muslim, Christian, Buddhist or an adherent of any other sect. Such designations are non—*sanātana-dharma.* A Hindu may change his faith to become a Muslim, or a Muslim may change his faith to become a Hindu, or a Christian may change his faith and so on. But in all circumstances the change of religious faith does not affect the eternal occupation of rendering service to others. The Hindu, Muslim or Christian in all circumstances is servant of someone. Thus, to profess a particular type of faith is not to profess one's *sanātana-dharma.* The rendering of service is *sanātana-dharma.*

Factually we are related to the Supreme Lord in service. The Supreme Lord is the supreme enjoyer, and we living entities are His servitors. We are created for His enjoyment, and if we participate in that eternal enjoyment with the Supreme Personality of Godhead, we become happy. We cannot become happy otherwise. It is not possible to be happy independently, just as no one part of the body can be happy without cooperating with the stomach. It is not possible for the living entity to be happy without rendering transcendental loving service unto the Supreme Lord.

In the *Bhagavad-gītā*, worship of different demigods or rendering service to them is not approved. It is stated in the Seventh Chapter, twentieth verse:

kāmais tais tair hṛta jñānāḥ
prapadyante 'nya-devatāḥ
taṁ taṁ niyamam āsthāya
prakṛtyā niyatāḥ svayā

"Those whose intelligence has been stolen by material desires surrender unto demigods and follow the particular rules and regulations of worship according to their own natures." Here it is plainly said that those who are directed by lust worship the demigods and not the Supreme Lord Kṛṣṇa. When we mention the name Kṛṣṇa, we do not refer to any sectarian name. Kṛṣṇa means the highest pleasure, and it is confirmed that the Supreme Lord is the reservoir or storehouse of all pleasure. We are all hankering after pleasure. *Ānanda-mayo 'bhyāsāt* (*Vedānta-sūtra* 1.1.12). The living entities, like the Lord, are full of consciousness, and they are after happiness. The Lord is perpetually happy, and if the living entities associate with the Lord, cooperate with Him and take part in His association, then they also become happy.

The Lord descends to this mortal world to show His pastimes in Vṛndāvana, which are full of happiness. When Lord Śrī Kṛṣṇa was in Vṛndāvana, His activities with His cowherd boyfriends, with His damsel friends, with the other inhabitants of Vṛndāvana and with the cows were all full of happiness. The total population of Vṛndāvana knew nothing but Kṛṣṇa. But Lord Kṛṣṇa even discouraged His father Nanda Mahārāja from worshiping the demigod Indra, because He wanted to establish the fact that people need not worship any demigod. They need only worship the Supreme Lord, because their ultimate goal is to return to His abode.

The abode of Lord Śrī Kṛṣṇa is described in the *Bhagavad-gītā*, Fifteenth Chapter, sixth verse:

na tad bhāsayate sūryo
na śaśāṅko na pāvakaḥ
yad gatvā na nivartante
tad dhāma paramaṁ mama

"That supreme abode of Mine is not illumined by the sun or moon, nor by fire or electricity. Those who reach it never return to this material world."

This verse gives a description of that eternal sky. Of course we have a material conception of the sky, and we think of it in relationship to the sun, moon, stars and so on, but in this verse the Lord states that in the eternal sky there is no need for the sun nor for the moon nor electricity or fire of any kind because the spiritual sky is already illuminated by the *brahmajyoti,* the rays emanating from the Supreme Lord. We are trying with difficulty to reach other planets, but it is not difficult to understand the abode of the Supreme Lord. This abode is referred to as Goloka. In the *Brahma-saṁhitā* (5.37) it is beautifully described: *goloka eva nivasaty akhilātma-bhūtaḥ*. The Lord resides eternally in His abode Goloka, yet He can be approached from this world, and to this end the Lord comes to manifest His real form, *sac-cid-ānanda-vigraha*. When He manifests this form, there is no need for our imagining what He looks like. To discourage such imaginative speculation, He descends and exhibits Himself as He is, as Śyāmasundara. Unfortunately, the less intelligent deride Him because He comes as one of us and plays with us as a human being. But because of this we should not consider the Lord one of us. It is by His omnipotency that He presents Himself in His real form before us and displays His pastimes, which are replicas of those pastimes found in His abode.

In the effulgent rays of the spiritual sky there are innumerable planets floating. The *brahmajyoti* emanates from the supreme abode, *Kṛṣṇaloka,* and the *ānanda-maya, cin-maya* planets, which are not material, float in those rays. The Lord says, *na tad bhāsayate sūryo na śaśāṅko na pāvakaḥ/ yad gatvā na nivartante tad dhāma paramaṁ mama.* One who can approach that spiritual sky is not required to descend again to the material sky. In the material sky, even if we approach the highest planet (Brahmaloka), what to speak of the moon, we will find the same conditions of life, namely birth, death, disease and old age. No planet in the material universe is free from these four principles of material existence.

The living entities are traveling from one planet to another, but it is not that we can go to any planet we like merely by a mechanical arrangement. If we desire to go to other planets, there is a process for going there. This is also mentioned: *yānti deva-vratā devān pitṝn yānti pitṛ-vratāḥ.* No mechanical arrangement is necessary if we want interplanetary travel. The *Gītā* instructs: *yānti deva-vratā devān.* The moon, the sun and higher planets are called Svargaloka. There are three different statuses of planets: higher, middle and lower planetary systems. The earth belongs to the middle planetary system. *Bhagavad-gītā* informs us how to travel to the higher planetary systems (Devaloka) with a very simple formula: *yānti deva-vratā devān.* One need only worship the particular demigod of that particular planet and in that way go to the moon, the sun or any of the higher planetary systems.

Yet *Bhagavad-gītā* does not advise us to go to any of the planets in this material world, because even if we go to Brahmaloka, the highest planet, through some sort of mechanical contrivance by maybe traveling for forty thousand years (and who would live that long?), we will still find the material inconveniences of birth, death, disease and old age. But one who wants to approach the supreme planet, Kṛṣṇaloka, or any of the other planets within the spiritual sky, will not meet with these material inconveniences. Amongst all of the planets in the spiritual sky there is one supreme planet called Goloka Vṛndāvana, which is the original planet in the abode of the original Personality of Godhead Śrī Kṛṣṇa. All of this information is given in *Bhagavad-gītā,* and we are given through its instruction information how to leave the material world and begin a truly blissful life in the spiritual sky.

In the Fifteenth Chapter of the *Bhagavad-gītā,* the real picture of the material world is given. It is said there:

ūrdhva-mūlam adhaḥ-śākham
aśvatthaṁ prāhur avyayam
chandāṁsi yasya parṇāni
yas taṁ veda sa veda-vit

Here the material world is described as a tree whose roots are upwards and branches are below. We have experience of a tree whose roots are upward: if one stands on the bank of a river or any reservoir of water, he can see that the trees reflected in the water are upside down. The branches go downward and the roots upward. Similarly, this material world is a reflection of the spiritual world. The material world is but a shadow of reality. In the shadow there is no reality or substantiality, but from the shadow we can understand that there are substance and reality. In the desert there is no water, but the mirage suggests that there is such a thing as water. In the material world there is no water, there is no happiness, but the real water of actual happiness is there in the spiritual world.

The Lord suggests that we attain the spiritual world in the following manner (Bg. 15.5):

nirmāna-mohā jita-saṅga-doṣā
adhyātma-nityā vinivṛtta-kāmāḥ
dvandvair vimuktāḥ sukha-duḥkha-saṁjñair
gacchanty amūḍhāḥ padam avyayaṁ tat

That *padam avyayam,* or eternal kingdom, can be reached by one who is *nirmāna-moha.* What does this mean? We are after designations. Someone wants to become "sir," someone wants to become "lord," someone wants to become the president or a rich man or a king or something else. As long as we are attached to these designations, we are attached to the body, because designations belong to the body. But we are not these bodies, and realizing this is the first stage in spiritual realization. We are associated with the three modes of material nature, but we must become detached through devotional service to the Lord. If we are not attached to devotional service to the Lord, then we cannot become detached from the modes of material nature. Designations and attachments are due to our lust and desire, our wanting to lord it over the material nature. As long as we do not give up this propensity of lording it over material nature, there is no possibility of returning to the kingdom of the Supreme, the *sanātana-dhāma.* That eternal kingdom, which is never destroyed, can be approached by one who is not bewildered by the attractions of false material enjoyments, who is situated in the service of the Supreme Lord. One so situated can easily approach that supreme abode.

Elsewhere in the *Gītā* (8.21) it is stated:

avyakto 'kṣara ity uktas
tam āhuḥ paramāṁ gatim
yaṁ prāpya na nivartante
tad dhāma paramaṁ mama

Avyakta means unmanifested. Not even all of the material world is manifested before us. Our senses are so imperfect that we cannot even see all of the stars within this material universe. In Vedic literature we can receive much information about all the planets, and we can believe it or not believe it. All of the important planets are described in Vedic literatures, especially *Śrīmad-Bhāgavatam,* and the spiritual world, which is beyond this material sky, is described as *avyakta,* unmanifested. One should desire and hanker after that supreme kingdom, for when one attains that kingdom, he does not have to return to this material world.

Next, one may raise the question of how one goes about approaching that abode of the Supreme Lord. Information of this is given in the Eighth Chapter. It is said there:

anta-kāle ca mām eva
smaran muktvā kalevaram
yaḥ prayāti sa mad-bhāvaṁ
yāti nāsty atra saṁśayaḥ

"Anyone who quits his body, at the end of life, remembering Me, attains immediately to My nature; and there is no doubt of this." (Bg. 8.5) One who thinks of Kṛṣṇa at the time of his death goes to Kṛṣṇa. One must remember the form of Kṛṣṇa; if he quits his body thinking of this form, he surely approaches the spiritual kingdom. *Mad-bhāvam* refers to the supreme nature of the Supreme Being. The Supreme Being is *sac-cīd-ānanda-vigraha*—that is, His form is eternal, full of knowledge and bliss. Our present body is not *sac-cid-ānanda.* It is *asat,* not *sat.* It is not eternal; it is perishable. It is not *cit,* full of knowledge, but it is full of ignorance. We have no knowledge of the spiritual kingdom, nor do we even have perfect knowledge of this material world, where there are so many things unknown to us. The body is also *nirānanda;* instead of being full of bliss it is full of misery. All of the miseries we experience in the material world arise from the body, but one who leaves this body thinking of Lord Kṛṣṇa, the Supreme Personality of Godhead, at once attains a *sac-cid-ānanda* body.

The process of quitting this body and getting another body in the material world is also organized. A man dies after it has been decided what form of body he will have in the next life. Higher authorities, not the living entity himself, make this decision. According to our activities in this life, we either rise or sink. This life is a preparation for the next life. If we can prepare, therefore, in this life to get promotion to the kingdom of God, then surely, after quitting this material body, we will attain a spiritual body just like the Lord's.

As explained before, there are different kinds of transcendentalists—the *brahma-vādī, param-ātma-vādī* and the devotee—and, as mentioned, in the *brahmajyoti* (spiritual sky) there are innumerable spiritual planets. The number of these planets is far, far greater than all of the planets of this material world. This material world has been approximated as only one quarter of the creation (*ekāṁśena sthito jagat*). In this material segment there are millions and billions of universes with trillions of planets and suns, stars and moons. But this whole material creation is only a fragment of the total creation. Most of the creation is in the spiritual sky. One who desires to merge into the existence of the Supreme Brahman is at once transferred to the *brahmajyoti* of the Supreme Lord and thus attains the spiritual sky. The devotee, who wants to enjoy the association of the Lord, enters into the Vaikuṇṭha planets, which are innumerable, and the Supreme Lord by His plenary expansions as Nārāyaṇa with four hands and with different names like Pradyumna, Aniruddha and Govinda associates with him there. Therefore at the end of life the transcendentalists think either of the *brahmajyoti*, the Paramātmā or Supreme Personality of Godhead Śrī Kṛṣṇa. In all cases they enter into the spiritual sky, but only the devotee, or he who is in personal touch with the Supreme Lord, enters into the Vaikuṇṭha planets or the Goloka Vṛndāvana planet. The Lord further adds that of this "there is no doubt." This must be believed firmly. We should not reject that which does not tally with our imagination; our attitude should be that of Arjuna: "I believe everything that You have said." Therefore when the Lord says that at the time of death whoever thinks of Him as Brahman or Paramātmā or as the Personality of Godhead certainly enters into the spiritual sky, there is no doubt about it. There is no question of disbelieving it.

The *Bhagavad-gītā* (8.6) also explains the general principle that makes it possible to enter the spiritual kingdom simply by thinking of the Supreme at the time of death:

yaṁ yaṁ vāpi smaran bhāvaṁ
tyajaty ante kalevaram
taṁ tam evaiti kaunteya
sadā tad-bhāva-bhāvitaḥ

"Whatever state of being one remembers when he quits his present body, in his next life he will attain to that state without fail." Now, first we must understand that material nature is a display of one of the energies of the Supreme Lord. In the *Viṣṇu Purāṇa* (6.7.61) the total energies of the Supreme Lord are delineated:

viṣṇu-śaktiḥ parā proktā
kṣetra jñākhyā tathā parā
avidyā-karma-saṁjñānyā
tṛtīyā śaktir iṣyate

The Supreme Lord has diverse and innumerable energies which are beyond our conception; however, great learned sages or liberated souls have studied these energies and have analyzed them into three parts. All of the energies are of *viṣṇu-śakti*, that is to say they are different potencies of Lord Viṣṇu. The first energy is *parā*, transcendental. Living entities also belong to the superior energy, as has already been explained. The other energies, or material energies, are in the mode of ignorance. At the time of death either we can remain in the inferior energy of this material world, or we can transfer to the energy of the spiritual world. So the *Bhagavad-gītā* (8.6) says:

yaṁ yaṁ vāpi smaran bhāvaṁ
tyajaty ante kalevaram
taṁ tam evaiti kaunteya
sadā tad-bhāva-bhāvitaḥ

"Whatever state of being one remembers when he quits his present body, in his next life he will attain to that state without fail."

In life we are accustomed to thinking either of the material or of the spiritual energy. Now, how can we transfer our thoughts from the material energy to the spiritual energy? There are so many literatures which fill our thoughts with the material energy—newspapers, magazines, novels, etc. Our thinking, which is now absorbed in these literatures, must be transferred to the Vedic literatures. The great sages, therefore, have written so many Vedic literatures, such as the *Purāṇas*. The *Purāṇas* are not imaginative; they are historical records. In the *Caitanya-caritāmṛta (Madhya* 20.122) there is the following verse:

māyā-mugdha jīvera nāhi svataḥ kṛṣṇa-jñāna
jīvere kṛpāya kailā kṛṣṇa veda-purāṇa

The forgetful living entities or conditioned souls

have forgotten their relationship with the Supreme Lord, and they are engrossed in thinking of material activities. Just to transfer their thinking power to the spiritual sky, Kṛṣṇa-dvaipāyana Vyāsa has given a great number of Vedic literatures. First he divided the *Vedas* into four, then he explained them in the *Purāṇas*, and for less capable people he wrote the *Mahābhārata*. In the *Mahābhārata* there is given the *Bhagavad-gītā*. Then all Vedic literature is summarized in the *Vedānta-sūtra*, and for future guidance he gave a natural commentation on the *Vedānta-sūtra*, called *Śrīmad-Bhāgavatam*. We must always engage our minds in reading these Vedic literatures. Just as materialists engage their minds in reading newspapers, magazines and so many materialistic literatures, we must transfer our reading to these literatures which are given to us by Vyāsadeva; in that way it will be possible for us to remember the Supreme Lord at the time of death. That is the only way suggested by the Lord, and He guarantees the result: "There is no doubt."

tasmāt sarveṣu kāleṣu
mām anusmara yudhya ca
mayy arpita-mano-buddhir
mām evaiṣyasy asaṁśayaḥ

"Therefore, Arjuna, you should always think of Me in the form of Kṛṣṇa and at the same time continue your prescribed duty of fighting. With your activities dedicated to Me and your mind and intelligence fixed on Me, you will attain Me without doubt." (Bg. 8.7)

He does not advise Arjuna simply to remember Him and give up his occupation. No, the Lord never suggests anything impractical. In this material world, in order to maintain the body one has to work. Human society is divided, according to work, into four divisions of social order—*brāhmaṇa, kṣatriya, vaiśya* and *śūdra.* The *brāhmaṇa* class or intelligent class is working in one way, the *kṣatriya* or administrative class is working in another way, and the mercantile class and the laborers are all tending to their specific duties. In the human society, whether one is a laborer, merchant, administrator or farmer, or even if one belongs to the highest class and is a literary man, a scientist or a theologian, he has to work in order to maintain his existence. The Lord therefore tells Arjuna that he need not give up his occupation, but while he is engaged in his occupation he should remember Kṛṣṇa (*mām anusmara*). If he doesn't practice remembering Kṛṣṇa while he is struggling for existence, then it will not be possible for him to remember Kṛṣṇa at the time of death. Lord Caitanya also advises this. He says, *kīrtanīyaḥ sadā hariḥ:* one should practice chanting the names of the Lord always. The names of the Lord and the Lord are nondifferent. So Lord Kṛṣṇa's instructions to Arjuna to "remember Me" and Lord Caitanya's injunction to "always chant the names of Lord Kṛṣṇa" are the same instruction. There is no difference, because Kṛṣṇa and Kṛṣṇa's name are nondifferent. In the absolute status there is no difference between reference and referent. Therefore we have to practice remembering the

Lord always, twenty-four hours a day, by chanting His names and molding our life's activities in such a way that we can remember Him always.

How is this possible? The *ācāryas* give the following example. If a married woman is attached to another man, or if a man has an attachment for a woman other than his wife, then the attachment is to be considered very strong. One with such an attachment is always thinking of the loved one. The wife who is thinking of her lover is always thinking of meeting him, even while she is carrying out her household chores. In fact, she carries out her household work even more carefully so her husband will not suspect her attachment. Similarly, we should always remember the supreme lover, Śrī Kṛṣṇa, and at the same time perform our material duties very nicely. A strong sense of love is required here. If we have a strong sense of love for the Supreme Lord, then we can discharge our duty and at the same time remember Him. But we have to develop that sense of love. Arjuna, for instance, was always thinking of Kṛṣṇa; he was the constant companion of Kṛṣṇa, and at the same time he was a warrior. Kṛṣṇa did not advise him to give up fighting and go to the forest to meditate. When Lord Kṛṣṇa delineates the *yoga* system to Arjuna, Arjuna says that the practice of this system is not possible for him.

arjuna uvāca
yo 'yaṁ yogas tvayā proktaḥ
sāmyena madhusūdana
etasyāhaṁ na paśyāmi
cañcalatvāt sthitiṁ sthirām

"Arjuna said: O Madhusūdana, the system of *yoga* which You have summarized appears impractical and unendurable to me, for the mind is restless and unsteady." (Bg. 6.33)

But the Lord says:

yoginām api sarveṣāṁ
mad-gatenāntarātmanā
śraddhāvān bhajate yo māṁ
sa me yuktatamo mataḥ

"Of all *yogīs*, the one with great faith who always abides in Me, thinks of Me within himself, and renders transcendental loving service to Me is the most intimately united with Me in *yoga* and is the highest of all. That is My opinion." (*Bg. 6.47)* So one who thinks of the Supreme Lord always is the greatest *yogī*, the supermost *jñānī*, and the greatest devotee at the same time. The Lord further tells Arjuna that as a *kṣatriya* he cannot give up his fighting, but if Arjuna fights remembering Kṛṣṇa, then he will be able to remember Kṛṣṇa at the time of death. But one must be completely surrendered in the transcendental loving service of the Lord.

We work not with our body, actually, but with our mind and intelligence. So if the intelligence and the mind are always engaged in the thought of the Supreme Lord, then naturally the senses are also engaged in His service. Superficially, at least, the activities of the senses remain the same, but the consciousness is changed. The *Bhagavad-gītā* teaches one how to absorb the mind and intelligence in the thought of the Lord. Such absorption will enable one to transfer himself to the kingdom of the Lord. If the mind is engaged in Kṛṣṇa's service, then the senses are automatically engaged in His service. This is the art, and this is also the secret of *Bhagavad-gītā:* total absorption in the thought of Śrī Kṛṣṇa.

Modern man has struggled very hard to reach the moon, but he has not tried very hard to elevate himself spiritually. If one has fifty years of life ahead of him, he should engage that brief time in cultivating this practice of remembering the Supreme Personality of Godhead. This practice is the devotional process:

śravaṇaṁ kīrtanaṁ viṣṇoḥ
smaraṇaṁ pāda-sevanam
arcanaṁ vandanaṁ dāsyaṁ
sakhyam ātma-nivedanam
(*Śrīmad-Bhāgavatam* 7.5.23)

These nine processes, of which the easiest is *śravaṇam,* hearing the *Bhagavad-gītā* from the realized person, will turn one to the thought of the Supreme Being. This will lead to remembering the Supreme Lord and will enable one, upon leaving the body, to attain a spiritual body which is just fit for association with the Supreme Lord.

The Lord further says:

abhyāsa-yoga-yuktena
cetasā nānya-gāminā
paramaṁ puruṣaṁ divyaṁ
yāti pārthānucintayan

"He who meditates on Me as the Supreme Personality of Godhead, his mind constantly engaged in remembering Me, undeviated from the path, he, O Arjuna, is sure to reach Me." (Bg. 8.8)

This is not a very difficult process. However, one must learn it from an experienced person. *Tad vijñānārthaṁ sa gurum evābhigacchet:* one must approach a person who is already in the practice. The mind is always flying to this and that, but one must practice concentrating the mind always on the form of the Supreme Lord, Śrī Kṛṣṇa, or on the sound of His name. The mind is naturally restless, going hither and thither, but it can rest in the sound vibration of Kṛṣṇa. One must thus meditate on *paramaṁ puruṣam,* the Supreme Personality of Godhead in the spiritual kingdom, the spiritual sky, and thus attain Him. The ways and the means for ultimate realization, ultimate attainment, are stated in the *Bhagavad-gītā,* and the doors of this knowledge are open for everyone. No one is barred out. All classes of men can approach Lord Kṛṣṇa by thinking of Him, for hearing and thinking of Him is possible for everyone.

The Lord further says (Bg. 9.32–33):

māṁ hi pārtha vyapāśritya
ye 'pi syuḥ pāpa-yonayaḥ
striyo vaiśyās tathā śūdrās
te 'pi yānti parāṁ gatim

kiṁ punar brāhmaṇāḥ puṇyā
bhaktā rājarṣayas tathā

anityam asukhaṁ lokam
imaṁ prāpya bhajasva mām

Thus the Lord says that even a merchant, a fallen woman or a laborer or even human beings in the lowest status of life can attain the Supreme. One does not need highly developed intelligence. The point is that anyone who accepts the principle of *bhakti-yoga* and accepts the Supreme Lord as the *summum bonum* of life, as the highest target, the ultimate goal, can approach the Lord in the spiritual sky. If one adopts the principles enunciated in *Bhagavad-gītā,* he can make his life perfect and make a permanent solution to all the problems of life. This is the sum and substance of the entire *Bhagavad-gītā.*

In conclusion, *Bhagavad-gītā* is a transcendental literature which one should read very carefully. *Gītā-śāstram idaṁ puṇyaṁ yaḥ paṭhet prayataḥ pumān:* if one properly follows the instructions of *Bhagavad-gītā,* one can be freed from all the miseries and anxieties of life. *Bhaya-śokādi-varjitaḥ.* One will be freed from all fears in this life, and one's next life will be spiritual. (*Gītā-māhātmya* 1)

There is also a further advantage:

gītādhyāyana-śīlasya
prāṇāyama-parasya ca
naiva santi hi pāpāni
pūrva-janma-kṛtāni ca

"If one reads *Bhagavad-gītā* very sincerely and with all seriousness, then by the grace of the Lord the reactions of his past misdeeds will not act upon him." (*Gītā-māhātmya* 2) The Lord says very loudly in the last portion of *Bhagavad-gītā* (18.66):

sarva-dharmān parityajya
mām ekaṁ śaraṇaṁ vraja
ahaṁ tvāṁ sarva-pāpebhyo
mokṣayiṣyāmi mā śucaḥ

"Abandon all varieties of religion and just surrender unto Me. I shall deliver you from all sinful reactions. Do not fear." Thus the Lord takes all responsibility for one who surrenders unto Him, and He indemnifies such a person against all reactions of sins.

maline mocanaṁ puṁsāṁ
jala-snānaṁ dine dine
sakṛd gītāmṛta-snānaṁ
saṁsāra-mala-nāśanam

"One may cleanse himself daily by taking a bath in water, but if one takes a bath even once in the sacred Ganges water of *Bhagavad-gītā*, for him the dirt of material life is altogether vanquished." (*Gītā-māhātmya* 3)

gītā su-gītā kartavyā
kim anyaiḥ śāstra-vistaraiḥ
yā svayaṁ padmanābhasya
mukha-padmād viniḥsṛtā

Because *Bhagavad-gītā* is spoken by the Supreme Personality of Godhead, one need not read any other Vedic literature. One need only attentively and regularly hear and read *Bhagavad-gītā*. In the present age, people are so absorbed in mundane activities that it is not possible for them to read all the Vedic literatures. But this is not necessary. This one book, *Bhagavad-gītā,* will suffice, because it is the essence of all Vedic literatures and especially because it is spoken by the Supreme Personality of Godhead. *(Gītā-māhātmya* 4)

As it is said:

bhāratāmṛta-sarvasvaṁ
viṣṇu-vaktrād viniḥsṛtam
gītā-gaṅgodakaṁ pītvā
punarjanma na vidyate

"One who drinks the water of the Ganges attains salvation, so what to speak of one who drinks the nectar of *Bhagavad-gītā*? *Bhagavad-gītā* is the essential nectar of the *Mahābhārata,* and it is spoken by Lord Kṛṣṇa Himself, the original Viṣṇu." *(Gītā-māhātmya 5) Bhagavad-gītā* comes from the mouth of the Supreme Personality of Godhead, and the Ganges is said to emanate from the lotus feet of the Lord. Of course, there is no difference between the mouth and the feet of the Supreme Lord, but from an impartial study we can appreciate that *Bhagavad-gītā* is even more important than the water of the Ganges.

sarvopaniṣado gāvo
dogdhā gopāla-nandanaḥ
pārtho vatsaḥ su-dhīr bhoktā
dugdhaṁ gītāmṛtaṁ mahat

"This *Gītopaniṣad, Bhagavad-gītā,* the essence of all the *Upaniṣads,* is just like a cow, and Lord Kṛṣṇa, who is famous as a cowherd boy, is milking this cow. Arjuna is just like a calf, and learned scholars and pure devotees are to drink the nec-tarean milk of *Bhagavad-gītā.*" (*Gītā-māhātmya* 6)

ekaṁ śāstraṁ devakī-putra-gītam
eko devo devakī-putra eva
eko mantras tasya nāmāni yāni
karmāpy ekaṁ tasya devasya sevā
(*Gītā-māhātmya* 7)

In this present day, people are very much eager to have one scripture, one God, one religion, and one occupation. Therefore, *ekaṁ śāstraṁ devakī-putra-gītam:* let there be one scripture only, one common scripture for the whole world—*Bhagavad-gītā. Eko devo devakī-putra eva:* let there be one God for the whole world—Śrī Kṛṣṇa. *Eko mantras tasya nāmāni:* and one hymn, one *mantra,* one prayer—the chanting of His name: Hare Kṛṣṇa, Hare Kṛṣṇa, Kṛṣṇa Kṛṣṇa, Hare Hare/ Hare Rāma, Hare Rāma, Rāma Rāma, Hare Hare. *Karmāpy ekaṁ tasya devasya sevā:* and let there be one work only—the service of the Supreme Personality of Godhead.

ISKCON CENTERS AROUND THE WORLD

ISKCON is a world wide community of devotees of Krishna dedicated to the principles of bhakti-yoga. Classes are held in the evenings during the week, and a special feast and festival is held every Sunday afternoon. Write, call, or visit for further information.

NORTH AMERICA

CANADA

Montreal, Quebec—1626 Pie IX Boulevard, H1V 2C5/ Tel. (514) 521-1301 **Ottawa, Ontario**—212 Somerset St. E., K1N 6V4/ Tel. (613) 233-1884 **Regina, Saskatchewan**—1279 Retallack St., S4T 2H8/ Tel. (306) 525-1640 **Toronto, Ontario**—243 Avenue Rd., M5R 2J6/ Tel. (416) 922-5415 **Vancouver, B.C.**—5462 S.E. Marine Dr., Burnaby V5J 3G8/ Tel. (604) 433-9728

FARM COMMUNITY

Ashcroft, B.C.—Saranagati Dhama, Box 99, Ashcroft, B.C. V0K 1A0

RESTAURANTS

Toronto—Hare Krishna Dining Room (at ISKCON Toronto) **Vancouver**—Hare Krishna Buffet (at ISKCON Vancouver)

U.S.A.

Arcata, California—P.O. Box 4233, Arcata, CA / Tel. (707) 826-9219 **Atlanta, Georgia**—1287 Ponce de Leon Ave. N.E., 30306/ Tel. (404) 377- 8680 **Baltimore, Maryland**—200 Bloomsbury Ave., Catonsville 21228/ Tel. (301) 744-9537 **Boise, Idaho**—1615 Martha St., 83706/ Tel. (208) 344-427 **Boston, Massachusetts**—72 Commonwealth Ave., 02116/ Tel. (617) 247-8611 **Chicago, Illinois**—1716 W. Lunt Ave., 60626/ Tel. (312) 973-0900 **Cleveland, Ohio**—11206 Clifton Blvd., 44102/ Tel. (216) 651-6670 **Dallas, Texas**—5430 Gurley Ave., 75223/ Tel. (214) 827-6330 **Denver, Colorado**—1400 Cherry St., 80220/ Tel. (303) 333-5461 **Detroit, Michigan**—383 Lenox Ave., 48215/ Tel. (313) 824-6000 **Gurabo, Puerto Rico**—ISKCON, HC 1, Box 8440, 00658-9763/ Tel. (809) 737-5222
Gainesville, Florida—214 N.W. 14th St., 32603/ Tel. (904) 336-4183 **Honolulu, Hawaii**—51 Coelho Way, 96817/ Tel. (808) 595-3947 **Houston, Texas**—1320 W. 34th St., 77018/ Tel. (713) 686-4482 **Laguna Beach, California**—285 Legion St., 92651/ Tel. (714) 494-7029 **Lansing, Michigan**—1914 E. Michigan Ave., 48912/ Tel. (517) 484-2209 **Long Island, New York**—197 S. Ocean Ave., Freeport, 11520/ Tel. (516) 378-6184 **Los Angeles, California**—3764 Watseka Ave., 90034/ Tel. (213) 836-2676 **Miami, Florida**—3220 Virginia St., 33133/Tel. (305) 442-7218 **New Orleans, Louisiana**—2936 Esplanade Ave., 70119/ Tel. (504) 486-8605 **New York, New York**—305 Schermerhorn St., Brooklyn 11217/ Tel.(718) 855-6714 **Philadelphia, Pennsylvania**—51 W. Allens Lane, 19119/ Tel. (215) 247-4600 **Philadelphia, Pennsylvania**—529 South St., 19147/ Tel. (215) 829-0399 **St. Louis, Missouri**—3926 Lindell Blvd., 63108/ Tel. (314) 535-8085 **San Diego, California**—1030 Grand Ave., Pacific Beach 92109/ Tel. (619) 483-2500 **San Francisco, California**—84 Carl St., 94117/ Tel. (415) 753-8647 **San Francisco, California**—2334 Stuart St., Berkeley 94705/ Tel. (415) 644-1113 **Seattle, Washington**—1420 228th Ave. S.E., Issaquah 98027/ Tel. (206) 391-3293 **Tallahassee, Florida**—1323 Nylic St. (mail: P.O. Box 20224, 32304)/ Tel. (904) 681-9258 **Topanga, California**—20395 Callon Dr., 90290/ Tel. (213) 455-1658 **Towaco, New Jersey**—(mail: P.O. Box 109, 07082)/ Tel. (201) 299-0970 **Walla Walla, Washington**—314 E. Poplar, 99362/ Tel. (509) 529-9556 **Washington, D.C.**—10310 Oaklyn Dr., Potomac, Maryland 20854/ Tel. (301) 299-2100

FARM COMMUNITIES

Carriere, Mississippi (New Talavan)—Route 2, Box 449, 39426/ Tel. (601) 798-8533 **Gainesville, Florida (New Ramana-reti)**—Box 819, Alachua 32615/ Tel. (904) 462-9046 **Gurabo, Puerto Rico (New Govardhana Hill)**—(contact ISKCON Gurabo) **Hillsborough, North Carolina (New Goloka)**—Rt. 6, Box 701, 27278/ Tel. (919) 732-6492 **Mulberry, Tennessee (Murari-sevaka)**—Murari Project, Rt. No. 1, Box 146-A, 37359/ Tel. (615) 759-7331 **Port Royal, Pennsylvania (Gita-nagari)**—R.D. No. 1, Box 839, 17082/ Tel. (717) 527-4101

RESTAURANTS

Chicago—Govinda's Buffet (at ISKCON Chicago) **Boulder, Colorado**—917 Pleasant St., 80302 / Tel. (303) 444-7005 **Dallas**—Kalachandji's (at ISKCON Dallas) **Denver**—(at ISKCON Denver) **Detroit**—Govinda's (at ISKCON Detroit) / Tel. (313) 331-6740 **Laguna Beach**—Gauranga's (at ISKCON Laguna Beach) **Lansing, Michigan**—Govinda's Diners' Club (at ISKCON Lansing) **Los Angeles**—Govinda's, 9624 Venice Blvd., Culver City 90230/ Tel. (213) 836-1269 **Philadelphia**—Govinda's, 529 South St., 19147 / Tel. (215) 829-0077 **Provo, Utah**—Govinda's Buffet, 260 North University, 84601 /Tel. (801) 375-0404 **Santa Cruz, California**—Gauranga's, 503 Water St., 95060 / Tel. (408) 427-0294

EUROPE

GREAT BRITAIN AND NORTHERN IRELAND

Belfast, Northern Ireland—140 Upper Dunmurray Lane, Belfast/ Tel. (0232) 681328 **Birmingham, West Midlands**—84 Stanmore Rd., Edgebaston **Dublin, Eire**—Hare Krishna Centre, 3 Temple Lane, Dublin 2/ Tel. 353-1-6795887 **Leicester, England**—21 Thoresby St., North Evington, Leicester/ Tel. (0533)-762587 **Liverpool, England**—135 Northumberland St., Liverpool, L8 8AY/ Tel. (051)-709 9188 **Manchester, England**—20 Mayfield Road, Whalley Range, Manchester M16 8FT/ Tel. (061)-226 4416 **Newcastle upon Tyne, England**—21 Leazes Park Rd./Tel. (091)- 222-0150 **London, England (city)**—10 Soho St., London W1V 5FA / Tel. (71) 437-3662 **London, England (country)**—Bhaktivedanta Manor, Letchmore Heath, Watford, Hertfordshire WD2 8EP/ Tel. (092385) 7244 **Scotland**—Karuna Bhavan, Bankhouse Road, Lesmahagow, Lanarkshire/ Tel. (0555)-894790

FARM COMMUNITIES

Hare Krishna Island, N. Ireland—Derrylin, County Fermanagh, BT92 96N, N. Ireland/ Tel. (3657) 21512 **London, England**—(contact Bhaktivedanta Manor)

RESTAURANTS

London, England—Govinda's, 9–10 Soho St. / Tel. (71) 437-3662

ITALY

Bologna—Via Nazionale 124, 40065-Pianoro (BO)/ Tel. (51) 774-034 **Bergamo**—Villaggio Hare Krishna, Via Galileo Galilei, 41, 24040 Chignolo D'isola (BG)/ Tel. 035-490706 **Catania**—Via San Nicolo al Borgo 28, 95128 Catania, Sicily/ Tel. (95) 522-252 **Naples**—Via Vesuvio, N33, Ercolano LNA7/ Tel. (81) 739-0398 **Padua**—Via delle Granze 107, 35040

Loc. Camin (PD)/ Tel. (49) 760-007 **Rome**—Via di Tor Tre Teste 142, 00169 Roma/ Tel. (06) 262913

FARM COMMUNITY

Florence (Villa Vrindavan)—Via Communale degli Scopeti 108, S. Andrea in Percussina, San Cascian Val di Pesa (FI) 5002/Tel. (55) 820-054

RESTAURANTS

Milan—Govinda's, Via Valpetrosa 3/5, 20123 Milano / Tel. (2) 862-417 **Rome**—Govinda's, Via di San Simone 73/A, 00186 Roma/ Tel. (6) 654-1973

OTHER COUNTRIES

Amsterdam, Holland—Krishna Dham, 225 Ruysdaelkade, 1072 AW/ Tel.(020) 751 404 **Antwerp, Belgium**—184 Amerikalei 2000/ Tel. (03) 237-0037, 237-0038 **Athens, Greece**—Poseidonos 27, Ilioupoli, 16 345/ Tel. 01-993-7080 **Barcelona, Spain**—c/de L'Oblit, 67-08026/ (93) 347-9933 **Belgrade, Yugoslavia**—Vaisnavska vjerska zajednica, Sumatovacka 118, 11000 Beograd/ Tel. (0) 11/ 434-183 **Bellinzona, Switzerland**—New Nandagram, al Chiossascio, 6594 ContoneTI/Tel. 092-622747 **Berlin, W. Germany**—Bhakti Yoga Zentrum, Friedrichstrasse 31, 1000Berlin 61/ Tel. (030)2514372 **Brussels, Belgium**—49 rue Marche aux Poulets,1000 Bruxelles/ Tel. (02)513 86 05/04 **Budapest, Hungary**—M.K.T.H.K., J. Kalmar, Marton U. 52, 1038 Budapest **Copenhagen, Denmark**—Kongens Tvaerej 11, DK-2000 Frederiksberg/ Tel. (01) 86-85-81 **Durbuy, Belgium**—Chateau de Petit Somme, Durbuy 5482/ Tel. 086-322926 **Gothenburg, Sweden**—Grimmeredsvaegen 103, 421 69 Vaestra Froelunda/Tel. 031-290966 **Grodinge, Sweden**—Korsnas Gard, 14792 Grodinge/ Tel. 0753-29151 **Hamburg, W. Germany**—Holzbrucke 2a, 2000 Hamburg/ Tel. (040) 8503464 **Heidelberg, W. Germany**—Kurfuerstenalage 5, D-6900/ Tel. 06221 15101 **Helsinki, Finland**—Eljaksentie 9, 00370 Helsinki **Hoerup, W. Germany**—Neuhoerup 1, D-2391 Hoerup **Lisbon, Portugal**—Rua Fernao Lopes, 6, Cascais 2750 (mail: Apartado 2489, Lisboa 1112)/Tel. (11) 286 713 **Malmoe, Sweden**—Center for Vedisk Kultur, Remegentsgata 14, S-211 42 Malmoe/ Tel. (040) 127181 **Moscow, USSR**—Contact ISKCON Office of Soviet Affairs, Almviks Gard, 15300 Jarna, Sweden/ Tel. (46) 0755-52050 **Munich, W. Germany**—Brodstrasse 12, D-8000 Muenchen 82 **Oslo, Norway**—Senter for Krishnabevissthet, Skolestien 11, 0373 Oslo 3 **Paris, France**—31 Rue Jean Vacquier, 93160 Noisy le Grand/ Tel. 45921018; 43043263 **Prague, Czechoslovakia**—Hare Krishna, Na Nrazi 5, 18000 Praha 8 / Tel. 42-2-821438 **Pregrada, Yugoslavia**—Davor Bateli, Gorika 5/6, Pregrada / Tel. 38-49-73176 **Stockholm, Sweden**—Fridhemsgatan 22, 112 40 Stockholm/ Tel. 08-549002 **Turku, Finland**—ISKCON, Sairashuokeenkatu 8A1, 20140 Turku 14/Tel. (9) 21 308981 **Vienna, Austria**—Center for Vedic Studies, Rosenackerstrasse 26, 1170 Vienna/ Tel. (0222) 455830 **Warsaw, Poland**—Towarzystwo Swiadomosci Kryszny—Bhakti Yoga W PRL, 02-770 Warasawa130, skr. pocztowa 257 **Zurich, Switzerland**—Bergstrasse 54, 8030 Zuerich/ Tel. (01) 262-33-88 **Zurich, Switzerland**—Preyergrasse 16, CH-8001 Zuerich

FARM COMMUNITIES

Jandelsbrunn, W. Germany (Nava-Jiyada-Nrsimha-Ksetra)—Zielberg 20, D-8391/ Tel. 85831332 **Brihuega, Spain (New Vraja Mandala)**—(Santa Clara) Brihuega, Guadalajara/ Tel. (11)280018 **Denmark**—Gl. Kirikevej 3, 6650 Broerup/ Tel. 45-75-392921 **Jarna, Sweden**—Almviks Gard, 15300 Jarna/ Tel. (0755) 52050, (0755) 52073 **Roch d'Or, Switzerland**—The Gokula Project, Vacherie Dessous, Ch-2913 Roch d'Or/ Tel. 066-766160 **Valençay, France (New Mayapur)**—Luçay-Le-Male, 36 600/ Tel. (54) 40-23-53

RESTAURANTS

Malmoe, Sweden—Higher Taste, Amiralsgatan 6, S-211 55 Malmoe / Tel. (040) 970600 **Zurich, Switzerland**—Govinda's Restaurant, Preyergasse 16, 8001 Zurich / Tel. (01) 251-8859

AUSTRALASIA

AUSTRALIA

Adelaide—74 Semaphore Rd., Semaphore, S. A. 5019/Tel. (8) 493 200 **Brisbane**—95 Bank Road, Graceville, Q.L.D. (mail: P.O. Box 83, Indooroopilly 4068)/ Tel. (07) 379-5455 **Melbourne**—197 Danks St., Albert Park, Victoria 3206 (mail: P.O. Box 125)/ Tel. (03) 699-5122 **North Sydney**—180 Falcon St., N. Sydney, N.S.W. 2060 (mail: P.O. Box 220, Cammeray, N.S.W. 2060)/ Tel. (02) 955-6164 **Perth**—Sri Sri Gaura Nitai Perth Mandir, 144 Railway Parade (cnr. The Strand), Bayswater (mail: P.O. Box 102, Bayswater, W. A. 6053)/ Tel. (09) 370 1552, Fax. (09) 272 6636

Sydney—112 Darlinghurst Rd., Darlinghurst, N.S.W. 2010 (mail: P.O. Box 159, Kings Cross,N.S.W. 2011)/ Tel. (02) 3575162

FARM COMMUNITIES

Bambra (New Nandagram)—Oak Hill, Dean's Marsh Road, Bambra, VIC 3241/ Tel. (052)88738 **Millfield, N. S. W.**—New Gokula Farm, Lewis Lane (off Mt.View Rd. Millfield near Cessnock), N. S. W. / Tel. 049-981852 **Murwillumbah (New Govardhana)**—Tyalgum Rd., Eungella, via Murwillumbah N. S. W. 2484 (mail: P.O. Box 687)/ Tel. (066) 721903

RESTAURANTS

Adelaide—Crossways, 79 Hindley St., Adelaide, S.A. 5000 / Tel. (08) 231-5258 **Brisbane**—Crossways, First Floor, 99 Elisabeth Street **Melbourne**—Crossways, First Floor, 123 Swanston St., Melbourne, Victoria 3000 / Tel. (03) 650 2939 **Melbourne**—Gopal's, 139 Swanston St., Melbourne, Victoria 3000 / Tel. (03) 650-1578 **North Sydney**—Gopal's, 180 Falcon St., N. Sydney, N.S.W. 2060 / Tel. (02) 926164 **Perth**—Hare Krishna Food for Life, 129 Barrack St., Perth, WA 6000 / Tel. (09) 325 2168 **Sydney**—Govinda's Upstairs and Govinda's Take-away (both at ISKCON Sydney) / Tel. (075) 501642

NEW ZEALAND AND FIJI

Auckland, New Zealand (New Varshan)—Hwy. 18, Riverhead (next to Huapai Golf Course)(mail: R.D. 2, Kumeu, Auckland)/ Tel. (9) 4128075 **Christchurch, New Zealand**—83 Bealey Ave. (mail: P.O. Box 25-190 Christchurch)/ Tel. (3) 61965 **Labasa, Fiji**—Delailabasa (mail: Box 133)/ Tel. 82916 **Lautoka, Fiji**—5 Tavewa Ave. (mail: P.O. Box 125)/ Tel. 64112 **Rakiraki, Fiji**—Rewasa, Rakiraki (mail: P.O. Box 94243) **Suva, Fiji**—Nasinu 7 1/2 miles (P.O. Box 6376)/ Tel. 391-282 **Wellington, New Zealand**—6 Shotter St., Karori (mail: P.O. Box 2753, Wellington)/ Tel. (4) 764445

RESTAURANTS

Auckland, New Zealand—Gopal's, 1st Floor., Civic House, 291 Queen St. / Tel. 15 (9) 3034885 **Christchurch, New Zealand**—Gopal's, 143 Worcester St. / Tel. 67-035 **Lautoka, Fiji**—Gopal's, Corner of Yasawa St. & Naviti St. / Tel. 62990 **Suva, Fiji**—Gopal's, 18 Pratt St. / Tel. 62990 **Suva, Fiji**—Gopal's, 37 Cumming St. / Tel. 312259

AFRICA

Abeokuta, Nigeria—Ibadan Rd., Obantoko, behind NET

(mail: P.O. Box 5177) **Abidjan, Ivory Coast**—01 BP 8366, Abidjan

Accra, Ghana—582 Blk. 20, Odokor, Official Town (mail: P.O. Box 01568, Osu) **Buea, Cameroon**—Southwest Province (mail: c/o Yuh Laban Nkesah, P and T, VHS) **Cape Town, South Africa**—17 St. Andrews Rd., Rondebosch 7700/ Tel. (21) 689 1529 **Durban (Natal), S. Africa**—Chatsworth Circle, Chatsworth 4030 (mail: P.O. Box 56003)/ Tel. (31) 435-815 **Freetown, Sierra Leone**—13 Bright St., Brookfields (mail: P.O. Box 812, Freetown) **Johannesburg, South Africa**—14 Goldreid St., Hillbrow, Johannesburg 2001/Tel. (11) 666-2716 **Harare, Zimbabwe**—46 Crowhill Rd. (mail: P.O. Box 2090)/ Tel. 8877801 **Kitwe, Zambia**—3122 Gandhi Close, Buyantanshi (mail: P.O. Box 20242, Kitwe)/ Tel. 215-630 **Lagos, Nigeria**—No. 2 Murtala Mohammed International Airport Expressway, Mafaluku (mail: P.O. Box 8793, Lagos) **Phoenix, Mauritius**—Hare Krishna Land, Pont Fer, Phoenix (mail: P. O. Box 108, Quartre Bornes, Mauritius) / Tel. (230) 696-5804 **Mombasa, Kenya**—Hare Krishna House, Sauti Ya Kenya and Kisumu Rds. (mail P.O. Box 82224, Mombasa)/ Tel. 312248 **Nkawkaw, Ghana**—P.O. Box 69, Nkawkaw **Nairobi, Kenya**—Muhuroni Close, off West Nagara Rd. (mail: P.O. Box 28946, Nairobi)/ Tel. 744365

Port Harcourt, Nigeria—2 Eligbam Rd. (corner of Obana Obhan St.), G.R.A. II (mail: P.O. Box 4429, Trans Amadi) **Tokoradi, Ghana**—64 Windy Ridge (mail: P.O. Box 328) **Warri, Nigeria**—1 Ogunu St., Bendel Housing Estate, Ugborikoro (P.O. Box 1922, Warri)/ Tel. 053-230-262

FARM COMMUNITIES

Lusaka, Zambia—Plot 4/288 Chingololo Rd., Makeni (mail: P.O. Box 35658, Lusaka)/ Tel. 210-578

Mauritius (Vedic Farm)—ISKCON Vedic Farm, Hare Krishna Road, Beau Bois, Bon Accuel / Tel. 418-3955

RESTAURANT

Durban, S. Africa—Govinda's (contact ISKCON Durban)

ASIA

INDIA

Agartala, Tripura—Assam-Agartala Rd., Banamalipur, 799001 **Ahmedabad, Gujarat**—7, Kailas Society, Ashram Rd., 380 009/ Tel. 449935 **Bamanbore, Gujarat**—N.H. 88, Surendranagar Dist./ Tel. 97 **Bangalore, Karnataka**—Hare Krishna Hill, 1 'R' Block, Chord Road, Rajajinagar 560 010/ Tel. 359 856 **Baroda, Gujarat**—Hare Krishna Land, Gotri Rd., 390 015/ Tel. 326299 and 66499 **Bhayandar, Maharashtra**—Shivaji Chowk, Station Road, Bhayandar (West), Thane 401101/ Tel. 6982987 and 6982621 **Bhubaneswar, Orissa**—National Highway No. 5, Nayapali, 751 001/ Tel. 53125 **Bombay, Maharashtra**—Hare Krishna Land, Juhu 400 049/ Tel. 6206860 **Calcutta, W. Bengal**—3C Albert Rd., 700 017/ Tel. 443757, 434265, 446075 **Chandigarh, Punjab**—Hare Krishna Land, Dakshin Marg, Sector 36-B, 160 036/Tel. 44634 **Coimbatore, Tamil Nadu**—Padmam 387, VGR Puram, AlagenRoad–1, 641-001/Tel. 4597

Gauhati, Assam—Ulubari Charali, Gauhati 781 001/ Tel. 31208 **Guntur, A.P.**—Opp. Sivalayam, Peda Kakani 522 509 **Hardwar, U.P.**—Pahala Mala, Brittany Cottage, Kharkhari 249 401 (mail: P.O. Box 14) **Hyderabad, A.P.**—Hare Krishna Land, Nampally Station Rd., 500 001/ Tel. 551018, 552924 **Imphal, Manipur**—Hare Krishna Land, Airport Road, 795 001/ Tel. 21587 **Madras, Tamil Nadu**—59, Burkit Rd., T. Nagar, 600 017/ Tel. 443266 **Mayapur, W. Bengal**—Shree Mayapur Chandrodaya Mandir, P.O. Shree Mayapur Dham, Dist. Nadia/ Tel. 31(Swarup Ganj) **Moirang, Manipur**—Nongban Ingkhon, Tidim Rd./ Tel. 795133 **Nagpur, Maharashtra**—70 Hill Road, Ramnagar, 440 010/ Tel. 33513 **New Delhi**—M-119 Greater Kailash 1, 110 048/ Tel. 6412058, 6419701 **New Delhi**—14/63, Punjabi Bagh, 110 026/ Tel. 5410782 **Pandharpur, Maharashtra**—Hare Krishna Ashram, across Chandrabhaga River, Dist. Sholapur, 413 304 **Patna, Bihar**—Rajendra Nagar Road No. 12, 800 016/ Tel. 50765 **Pune, Maharashtra**—4 Tarapoor Rd., Camp, 411 001/ Tel. 60124 and 64003 **Secunderabad, A.P.**—9-1-1 St. John's Road, 500 026/Tel. 825232 **Silchar, Assam**—Ambikapatti, Silchar, Cachar Dist., 788004 **Siliguri, W. Bengal**—Gitalpara 734 401/ Tel. 26619

Surat, Gujarat—Rander Rd., Jahangirpura, 395 005/ Tel. 84215 **Tirupati, A.P.**—K.T. Road, Vinayaka Nagar 517 507/ Tel. 2285 **Trivandrum, Kerala**—T.C. 224/1485, WC Hospital Rd., Thycaud, 695 014/ Tel. 68197 **Udhampur, Jammu and Kashmir**—Prabhupada Nagar, Udhampur 182 101/Tel. 496 P.P. **Vrindavana, U.P.**—Krishna-Balaram Mandir, Bhaktivedanta Swami Marg, Raman Reti, Mathura Dist. 281 124/ Tel. (5664) 82478

FARM COMMUNITIES

Ahmedabad, Gujarat—Nityananda Seva Ashram, Odhav Rd, (near Octroi Naka), Odhav 382 410 Tel. 886 382 **Ahmedabad District, Gujarat**—Hare Krishna Farm, Katwada (contact: ISKCON Ahmedabad) **Assam**—Karnamadhu, Dist. Karimganj

Chamorshi, Maharashtra—78 Krishnanagar Dham, District Gadhachiroli, 442 603 **Hyderabad, A.P.**—P.O. Dabilpur Village, Medchal Tq., R.R. District, 501 401/ Tel. 552924 **Mayapur, W. Bengal**—(contact ISKCON Mayapur)

RESTAURANTS

Bombay, Maharashtra—Govinda's (at Hare Krishna Land)
Vrindavana—Krishna-Balaram Mandir Guesthouse

OTHER COUNTRIES

Bali, Indonesia—(Contact ISKCON Jakarta) **Bangkok, Thailand**—P.O. Box 15, Prakanong, Bangkok **Cagayan de Oro, Philippines**—30 Dahlia St., Ilaya Carmen, 900 Cagayan de Oro(c/o Sepulveda's Compound) **Chittagong, Bangladesh**—Caitanya Cultural Society, Sri Pundarik Dham, Mekhala, Hathazari Tel. 10 (city office and mail: 23 Nandan Kanan, Chittagong)/ Tel. 202219 **Colombo, Sri Lanka**—188 New Chetty St., Colombo 13/ Tel. 33325 **Hong Kong**—27 Chatam Road South, 6/F, Kowloon/ Tel. 3 7396818 **Iloilo City, Philippines**—13-1-1 Tereos St., La Paz, Iloilo City Iloilo/ Tel. 73391 **Jakarta, Indonesia**—P.O. Box 2694, Jakarta 10001 **Kathmandu, Nepal**—Vishnu Gaun Panchayat Ward No. 2, Budhanilkantha/ Tel. 4-10368 **Kuala Lumpur, Malaysia**—Lot 9901, Jalan Awan Jawa, Taman Yarl, off 5 1/2 Mile, Jalan Kelang Lama, Petaling/ Tel. 7830172 **Manila, Philippines**—170 R. Fernandez, San Juan, Metro Manila/ Tel. 707410 **Osafiya, Israel**—Hare Krishna, Osafiya 30900/Tel. 4-391150 **Taipei, Taiwan**—(mail: c/o ISKCON Hong Kong) **Tehran, Iran**—Keshavarz-Dehkedeh Ave., Kamran St. No. 58/ Tel. 658870 **Tel Aviv, Israel**—57 Frishman St., POB 48163, Tel Aviv 61480/ Tel. (03) 246325 **Tokyo, Japan**—2-41-12 Izumi, Suginami-ku, Tokyo T168/ Tel. (3) 327-1541

FARM COMMUNITIES

Bogor, Indonesia—Govinda Kunja (contact ISKCON Jakarta) **Cebu, Philippines (Hare Krishna Paradise)**—231 Pagsabungan Rd., Basak, Mandaue City/ Tel. 83254 **Perak, Malaysia**—Jalan Sungai Manik, 36000 Teluk Intan, Perak

RESTAURANTS

Cebu, Philippines—Govinda's, 26 Sanchiangko St. **Hong Kong**—The Higher Taste Vegetarian Dining Club (at ISKCON

Hong Kong) **Kuala Lumpur, Malaysia**—Govinda's, 16-1 Jalan Bunus Enam Masjid, India/Tel. 03-2986785

LATIN AMERICA

BRAZIL

Belem, PA—Av. Gentil Bittencourt, 1002–Nazare, CEP 66040 **Belo Horizonte, MG**—Rua St. Antonio, 45, Venda Nova, CEP 31510 **Brazilia, DF**—Q. 706-Sul, Bloco C, Casa 29, HIGS, CEP 70350/ Tel. (061) 242-7579 **Curitiba, PR**—Rua Jornalista Caio Machado, 291, B. Sta. Quiteria, CEP 80320 **Florianopolis, SC**—Rua 14 de julho, 922, Estreito, CEP 88075 **Fortaleza, CE**—Rua Jose Laurenço, 2114, Aldeota, CEP 60115 **Goiania, GO**—Rua C-60, Quadra 123, Lt-11, Setor Sudoeste, CEP 74305 **Manaus, AM**—Avenida 7 de Setembro, 1599, Centro, CEP 69003/ Tel: (092) 232-0202 **Pitajui, SP**—Av. Brazil, 306, CEP 16600 **Porto Alegre, RS**—Rua Tomas Flores, 331, Bomfim, CEP 90210 **Recife, PE**—Rua Reverendo Samuel Falcao, 75, Madalena, CEP 50710 **Rio de Janeiro, RJ**—Rua Armando Coelho de Freitas, 108, Barra da Tijuca, CEP 22620 **Salvador, BA**—Rua Alvaro Adorno, 17, Brotas, CEP 40240/ Tel: (071) 244-1072 **Santos, SP**—Rua Nabuco de Araujo, 151, Embare, CEP 11025/ Tel. (0132) 38-4655 **Sao Paulo, SP**—Avenida Angelica, 2583, Consolaçao, CEP 01227/ Tel. (011) 59-7352

FARM COMMUNITIES

Caruaru, PE—Comunidade Nova Vrajadhama, Distrito de Murici (mail: CP. 283, CEP 55100) **Pindamonhangaba, SP (Nova Gokula)**—Comunidade Nova Gokula, Barrio do Ribeirao Grande (mail: Caixa Postal 067 Pindamonhangaba, SP, CEP 12400)

RESTAURANT

Belem, Para (Shri Krishna Prasada)—Av. Gentil Bittencourt, Passagem Mac Dowell, 96 (entre Dr. Moraise Benjamin Constant / Tel (091) 222-1886

MEXICO

Guadalajara—Pedro Moreno 1791, Sector Juarez, Jalisco/ Tel. 26-12-78 **Mexico City**—Gobernador Tiburcio Montiel No. 45, Col. San Miguel Chapultepec, C.P. 11850, Mexico D.F. **Monterrey**—Zaragoza 1007, nte. Zona centro/ Tel. 74-69-76 **Tijuana**— Mutualismo 516 Primero C **Vera Cruz**—Calle 3, Carebelas No. 784, Fraccionamienito Reforma/ Tel. 50759

FARM COMMUNITY

La Primavera, Jalisco —(contact ISKCON Guadalajara)

PERU

Arequipa—Jerusalen 402/ Tel. 229523 **Cuzco**—San Juan de Dios 285 **Lima**—Pasaje Solea 101 Santa Maria-Chosica/ Tel. 910891 **Lima**—Schell 634 Miraflores **Lima**—Av. Garcilazo de la Vega 1670-1680/Tel. 259523

FARM COMMUNITY

Hare Krishna-Correo De Bella Vista—DPTO De San Martin

RESTAURANTS

Arequipa—(at ISKCON Arequipa) **Cuzco**—Espaderos 128 **Lima**—Schell 634 Miraflores

OTHER COUNTRIES

Asuncion, Paraguay—Centro Bhaktivedanta, Alberdi 1603 esq. 4ta., Asuncion/ Tel. 595-21-70066 **Bahia Blanca, Argentina**—Centro de Estudios Vedicos, F. Sanches 233, (8000) Bahia Blanca **Bogota, Colombia**—Calle 63A, #10-62, Chapinero/ Tel. 249-5797 **Bogota, Colombia**—Transversal 1a, #56-22, Alto Chapinero/ Tel. 255-8742 **Buenos Aires, Argentina**—Centro Bhaktivedanta, Andonaegui 2054, (1431)/Tel. 5155 **Cali, Colombia**—Avenida 2 EN, #24N-39/ Tel. 68-88-53 **Caracas, Venezuela**—Avenida Berlin, Quinta Tia Lola, La California Norte/Tel: (58-2) 225463 **Christ Church, Barbados**—31 Goodland Park/ Tel. (809) 42-84209 **Cochabamba, Bolivia**—Av. Heroinas E-0435 Apt. 3 (mail: P. O. Box 2070, Cochabamba

Concepcion, Chile—Nonguen, 588/ Tel. 23150 **Cordoba, Argentina**—Montevideo 950, Paso de los Andes/ Tel. (051) 262229 **Crabwood Creek, Guyana**—Grant 1803, Sec. D, Corentyne, Berbice **Cuenca, Ecuador**—Entrada de Las Pencas 1– Avenida de Las Americas/ Tel: (593-7) 825211 **Essequibo Coast, Guyana**—New Navadvipa Dham, Mainstay, Essequibo Coast **Georgetown, Guyana**—24 Uitvlugt Front, West Coast Demerara **Guatemala, Guatemala**—Apartado Postal 1534 **Guayaquil, Ecuador**— 6 de Marzo 226 y V. M. Rendon/Tel. (593-4) 308412 y 309420 **La Paz, Bolivia**—P. O. Box 10278, Miraflores, La Paz **Montevideo, Uruguay**—Centro de Bhakti-Yoga, Pablo de Maria 1427, Montevideo/ Tel. 598-2484551 **Panama, Republic of Panama**—Via las Cumbres, entrada Villa Zaita, frente a INPSA No. 1(mail: P.O. Box 6-29-54, Panama)

Pereira, Colombia—Carrera 5a, #19-36 **Quito, Ecuador**—Inglaterra y Amazonas **Rosario, Argentina**—Centro de Bhakti-Yoga, Paraguay 556, (2000)Rosario/Tel. 54-41-252630 **San Jose, Costa Rica**—Centro Cultural Govinda, 235 mtrs. norte del Banco Anglo, San Pedro (mail: Apdo. 166,100)/ Tel. 34-1218

San Salvador, El Salvador—Avenida Universitaria 1132, Media Quadra al sur de la Embajada Americana, San Salvador (mail: P.O. Box 1506)/ Tel. 25-96-17 **Santiago, Chile**—Carrera 330/ Tel. 698-8044 **Santo Domingo, Dominican Republic**—Calle Cayetano Rodriquez No. 254 **Trinidad and Tobago, West Indies**—Orion Drive, Debe/ Tel. 647-739 **Trinidad and Tobago, West Indies**—Prabhupada Ave. Longdenville, Chaguanas

FARM COMMUNITIES

Argentina (Bhaktilata Puri)—Casilla de Correo No 77, 1727 Marcos Paz, Pcia. Bs.As., Republica Argentina **Bolivia**—Contact ISKCON Cochabamba **Colombia (Nueva Mathura)**—Cruzero del Guali, Municipio de Caloto, Valle del Cauca Tel. 612688 en Cali **Ecuador (Nueva Mayapur)**—Ayampe (near Guayaquil) **Guyana**—Seawell Village, Corentyne, East Berbice **Guyaquil, Ecuador**—(Contact ISKCON Guyaquil) **San Jose, Costa Rica**—Granja Nueva Goloka Vrindavana, Carretera a Paraiso, de la entrada del Jardin Lancaster (por Calle Concava), 200 metros as sur (mano derecha)Cartago (mail: Apdo. 166, 1002)/ Tel. 51-6752 **San Salvador, El Salvador**—Carretera a Santa Ana, Km. 34, Canton Los Indios, Zapotitan, Dpto. de La Libertad

RESTAURANTS

Cochabamba, Bolivia—Gopal Restaurant, calle Espana N-0250 (Galeria Olimpia), Cochabamba(mail: P. O. Box 2070, Cochabamba **Guatemala, Guatemala**—Callejor Santandes a una cuadra abajo de Guatel, Panajachel Solola **Quito, Ecuador**—(contact ISKCON Quito) **San Salvador, El Salvador**—25 Avenida Norte 1132 **Santa Cruz, Bolivia**—Snack Govinda, Av. Argomosa (1ero anillo),

Bhagavad-gītā As It Is

The world's most popular edition of a timeless classic.

Throughout the ages, the world's greatest minds have turned to the *Bhagavad-gītā* for answers to life's perennial questions. Renowned as the jewel of India's spiritual wisdom, the *Gītā* summarizes the profound Vedic knowledge concerning man's essential nature, his environment, and ultimately his relationship with God. With more than fifty million copies sold in twenty languages, *Bhagavad-gītā As It Is*, by His Divine Grace A. C. Bhaktivedanta Swami Prabhupāda, is the most widely read edition of the *Gītā* in the world. It includes the original Sanskrit text, phonetic transliterations, word-for-word meanings, translation, elaborate commentary, and many full-color illustrations.

	Pocket	Vinyl	Hard	Deluxe
US	$3.90	$8.50	$10.30	$18.00
UK	£3.00	£5.25	£7.95	£13.95
AUS		$11.00	$14.00	$28.00

The Journey of Self-Discovery

In this collection of illuminating conversations and lectures, Śrīla Prabhupāda leads the reader to a deeper awareness of the self—and the Self.

283 pages

**Soft / US: $4.00; UK: £2.50;
AUS: $5.00**
**Hard / US: $9.95; UK: £7.50;
AUS: $12.00**

A Second Chance

The Story of a Near-Death Experience

As the sinful Ajāmila lay on his deathbed, he was terrified to see three fierce humanlike creatures coming to drag him out of his dying body for punishment. Surprisingly, he was spared. How? You'll find out in the pages of *A Second Chance.*

220 pages

**Soft / US: $4.00; UK: £2.50;
AUS: $5.00**
**Hard / US: $9.95; UK: £7.50;
AUS: $12.00**

Great Vegetarian Dishes

Featuring over 100 stunning full-color photos, this new book is for spiritually aware people who want the exquisite taste of Hare Kṛṣṇa cooking without a lot of time in the kitchen. The 240 international recipes were tested and refined by world-famous Hare Kṛṣṇa chef Kūrma dāsa.

240 recipes, 192 pages, coffeetable size hardback

US: $19.95; UK: £15.95; AUS: $24.95

The Hare Krishna Book Of Vegetarian Cooking

A colorfully illustrated, practical cookbook that not only helps you prepare authentic Indian dishes at home, but also teaches you about the ancient tradition behind India's world-famous vegetarian cuisine.

130 kitchen-tested recipes, 300 pages, hardback

US: $11.60; UK: £8.95; AUS: $15.00

The Higher Taste

A Guide to Gourmet Vegetarian Cooking and a Karma-Free Diet

Illustrated profusely with black-and-white ink drawings and eight full-color plates, this popular volume contains over 60 tried and tested international recipes, together with the why's and how's of the Kṛṣṇa conscious vegetarian life-style.

Softbound, 176 pages

US: $1.99; UK: £1.00; AUS: $2.00

Rāja-Vidyā: The King of Knowledge

In this book we learn why knowledge of Kṛṣṇa is absolute and frees the soul from material bondage.

Softbound, 128 pages

US: $1.00; UK: £1.00; AUS: $2.00

Easy Journey to Other Planets

One of Śrīla Prabhupāda's earliest books, *Easy Journey* describes how *bhakti-yoga* enables us to transfer ourselves from the material to the spiritual world.

Softbound, 96 pages

US: $1.00; UK: £1.00; AUS: $2.00

Beyond Birth and Death

What is the self? Can it exist apart from the physical body? If so, what happens to the self at the time of death? What about reincarnation? Liberation? *Beyond Birth and Death* answers these intriguing questions, and more.

Softbound, 96 pages

US: $1.00; UK: £1.00; AUS: $2.00

The Perfection of Yoga

A lucid explanation of the psychology, techniques, and purposes of *yoga;* a summary and comparison of the different *yoga* systems; and an introduction to meditation.

Softbound, 96 pages

US: $1.00; UK: £1.00; AUS: $2.00

Message of Godhead

An excerpt: "The influences of various people, places, and times have led us to designate ourselves as Hindus, Muslims, Christians, Buddhists, Socialists, Bolsheviks, and so forth. But when we attain transcendental knowledge and are established in *sanātana-dharma,* the actual, eternal religion of the living entity—the spirit soul—then and then only can we attain real, undeniable peace, prosperity, and happiness in the world."

Softbound, 68 pages

US: $1.00; UK: £1.00; AUS: $2.00

Keep in touch . . .

- ❒ Please send me a free information package, including the small booklet *Kṛṣṇa, the Reservoir of Pleasure* and a catalog of available books.
- ❒ Bhagavad-gītā As It Is [__Pocket __Vinyl __Hard __Deluxe]
- ❒ The Journey of Self-Discovery [__Hardbound __Softbound]
- ❒ A Second Chance [__Hardbound __Softbound]
- ❒ Great Vegetarian Dishes
- ❒ The Hare Krishna Book of Vegetarian Cooking
- ❒ The Higher Taste
- ❒ Rāja-Vidyā: The King of Knowledge
- ❒ Easy Journey to Other Planets
- ❒ Beyond Birth and Death
- ❒ The Perfection of Yoga
- ❒ Message of Godhead

Please send me the above books. I enclose $/£______________ to cover the cost and understand that the prices given include postage and packaging.

Name____
PLEASE PRINT

Address____

City__________________________ State____Zip______________

Mail this form to:

In Europe: The Bhaktivedanta Book Trust, P.O. Box 324, Borehamwood, Herts. WD6 1NB, U.K.

In North America: The Bhaktivedanta Book Trust, 3764 Watseka Ave., Los Angeles, CA 90034, U.S.A.

In Australasia: The Bhaktivedanta Book Trust, P.O. Box 262, Botany, N.S.W. 2019, Australia